SPEEDWEALTH™

"How To Make A Million
In Your Own Business In
3 Years Or Less."

BY T. HARV EKER

T. HARV EKER WENT FROM ZERO TO MILLIONAIRE
IN ONLY 2 1/2 YEARS. NOW YOU CAN TOO!

DEDICATION

This book is dedicated to my wife, Rochelle, my children, Maddi and Jesse, and my parents, Sam and Sara, without whom this book and my incredibly wonderful life would not be possible.

Special thanks to my entire team at Peak Potentials Training for all of their love, help and support.

And to all the people who have read my books, listened to my tapes and CD's and attended my workshops. Thank you for "showing up." Without you, I could not fulfill my life purpose.

All my love,

T. Harv Eker

First published in the United States of America.

DISCLAIMER

The advice contained in this material might not be suitable for everyone. The author designed the information to present his opinion about the subject matter. The reader must carefully investigate all aspects of any business decision before committing him—or herself. The author obtained the information contained herein from sources he believes to be reliable and from his own personal experience, but he neither implies nor intends any guarantee of accuracy. The author is not in the business of giving legal, accounting, or any other type of professional advice. Should the reader need such advice, he or she must seek services from a competent professional. The author particularly disclaims any liability, loss or risk taken by individuals who directly or indirectly act on the information contained herein. The author believes the advice presented here is sound, but readers cannot hold him responsible for either the actions they take or the result of those actions.

Published by Peak Potentials Publishing
Printed in Canada
Design by Suzanne Burr

1st Revision: April 2001
2nd Revision: February 2005
7th Printing: February 2006
ISBN 0-968-9855-0-5

MEET THE AUTHOR

T. Harv Eker

Financial Philosophy:

"If you're going to work hard anyway, you might as well get rich...and the quicker the better!"

"Forget theoretical advice!" T. Harv Eker's message comes direct from the firing lines of the "real" world. Described as a unique blend of "street-smarts with heart," Eker is one of North America's foremost business and personal success coaches. Having owned 17 businesses by the time he was 30, he uses hard-hitting, straight talk to pinpoint the critical elements that make the difference between success and failure.

Eker specializes in using the "Rags to Riches" approach. He has a knack for starting with little and earning large amounts of money, quickly. His passion is teaching others to do the same!

Starting with an initial investment of just $2000, he opened one of the first retail fitness stores in all of North America. In only 2 1/2 years, he expanded to 10 locations and then sold half the company shares to the H.J. Heinz Corporation (the ketchup people) for $1.6 million.

Eker is president of Peak Potentials Training, the fastest growing personal development company in North America. Eker is also author of the book, *Secrets of The Millionaire Mind,* and several highly-acclaimed seminars and camps. Over 250,000 participants have come from all over the world to attend T. Harv Eker's seminars.

A graduate from the "school of hard knocks," Eker shares the "ups and downs" of his own journey toward the ultimate combination of money, meaning and happiness. His students put it best, "T. Harv Eker makes success simple!"

Enjoy and prosper!

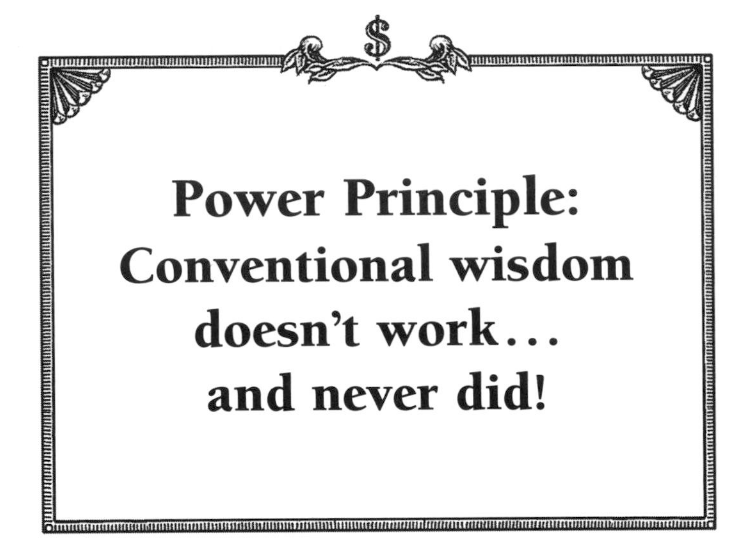

**Power Principle:
Conventional wisdom
doesn't work...
and never did!**

SPEEDWEALTH

Would you like to earn a lot of money?

Would you like to earn a lot of money . . . Quickly?

If so, you are in the right place. I am about to introduce you to a dynamic new business system that will allow you to create wealth faster than you may have ever dreamed possible.

My name is T. Harv Eker. I am the author of sixteen best-selling books, audio programs, and home learning courses in the areas of money, business and personal success. The groundbreaking book you have in your hands is my timeless and powerful program, "SpeedWealth", and I'd like to share it with you as a gift. I call it a "gift" because it has completely transformed my life, and the lives of thousands of others. I know it can do the same for you. Let me suggest you take a few moments right now to sit down, relax and read every word of this invaluable book. I assure you it will be well worth your time.

SpeedWealth is a step-by-step system for making a million dollars or more in your own business in 3 years or less, and <u>enjoying the journey</u> along the way!

Let me warn you. If you're expecting complex formulas, you are in for a surprise. The SpeedWealth methods are extremely simple, but they make people rich!

The SpeedWealth system is for people who already own a business, for people who want to own a business, and for people who have a job now, but want the security of "knowing" they can succeed on their own if they leave their job or it leaves them! It's for anyone who is tired of struggling for money and wants to become financially free, once and for all.

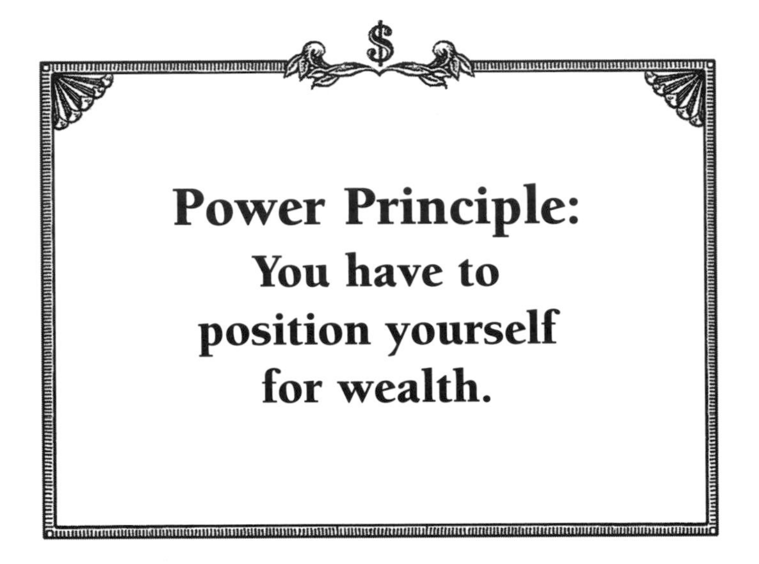

Power Principle:

You have to position yourself for wealth.

Do you have to own your own business in order for the SpeedWealth system to work? In a word, yes! Unfortunately, many people are still being sucked in by the old conventional wisdom, "Go to school, get good grades, get a good job, work hard and everything will be O.K." You don't have to be a rocket scientist to recognize that method doesn't work and never did. Notice, 85% of the population never becomes financially independent. I have nothing against having a job, but for most people, the acronym of J.O.B., "Just Over Broke," is accurate.

The key is "Positioning." Most people don't realize...

You have to position yourself for wealth.

Dreaming about making a million dollars in a job is like trying to see the ocean from the middle of Nebraska. You're just not in the right place for it.

If you're one of the few people who saves money and invests it in a compound interest savings account, that's good, but not good enough! Today's interest rates are about the lowest they've been in a decade. As for getting rich in real estate, that party is over too!

That leaves owning your own business as the last bastion remaining where creating wealth, especially quickly, is even possible. That's how I did it, and that's how you can do it too.

From Business Dunce To Business Wiz In
17 "Not-So-Easy" Lessons.

Like many people, I've tried anything and everything to "make it." In fact, I've actually owned 17 different businesses.

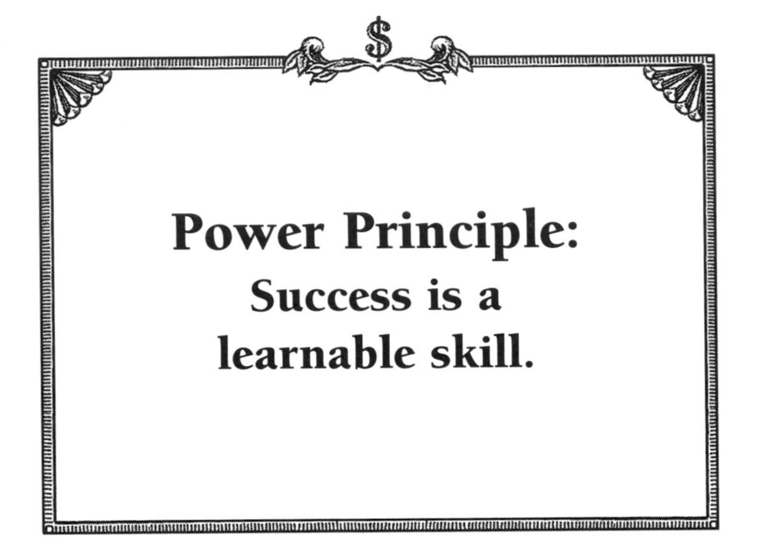
Power Principle:
Success is a
learnable skill.

My early business career was a disaster. I lost more money than I made. But one thing I always believed, was that . . .

Success is a learnable skill.

So I became the ultimate information junkie. I read every book, listened to every tape, and went to every success seminar I could find. Sure enough, things began to change. I got good at making money. Unfortunately, I was even better at spending it.

I had a choice: Earn much more or live on much less. That's when I made a conscious decision to become a millionaire – and the faster the better. I realized to achieve this goal, I would have to do something radically different from what I was doing before. A multi-millionaire acquaintance kept telling me, "If someone is doing better than you, it's because they know something you don't." So I decided to learn even more and devoted the next six months to analyzing the strategies and tactics of the world's greatest entrepreneurs — those who were making it big and fast. I pinpointed eight critical steps virtually every business that had achieved success quickly had in common. I named this system "SpeedWealth" and put it to the test. I borrowed $2,000 from my Visa card (my previous spending habits had totally dried up my bank account) and used the system to open one of the first retail fitness stores in all of North America. It was called Fitnessland. The results were "staggering." The SpeedWealth strategies allowed me to open 10 stores in only 2 1/2 years and then sell half my shares to the H.J. Heinz Corporation (the ketchup people), for $1.6 million.

The SpeedWealth system worked a money miracle for me and it can work one for you too. But first you have to learn it!

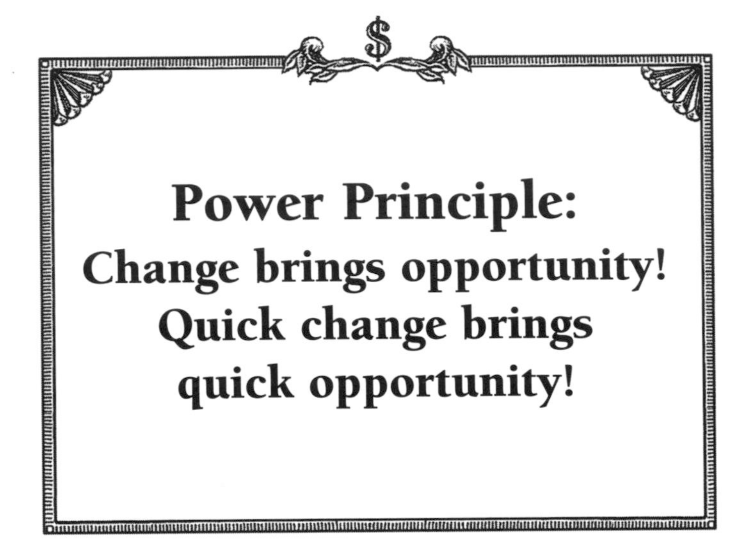

Power Principle:
Change brings opportunity!
Quick change brings
quick opportunity!

SPEEDWEALTH PRINCIPLE # 1: DEVELOP A SPEEDWEALTH MINDSET

Would you agree that your beliefs determine your actions? To have a SpeedWealth mindset you must believe the following two statements: 1. Getting rich quickly is feasible. 2. Getting rich quickly is feasible for <u>you</u>.

There's a lot of skepticism about "making money fast," but I think "Get Rich Quick" has gotten a bad rap! In the past, society has labeled those who wanted to create wealth quickly as "dreamers," "greedy," or "scam artists." But, several thousand people, including me, have gotten rich quickly and legitimately. There's not only nothing wrong with "making money fast," it is the wave of the future! The fact is, right now is the greatest time in history to create wealth quickly in your own business. Today, more and more fortunes are being made with lightening speed, and with good reason.

The world is changing quickly, technology is changing quickly, markets are changing quickly and people's interests are changing quickly.

Change brings opportunity!
Quick change brings quick opportunity!

Every time there is a change in technology, law, social interest, style, the market or the latest business buzzword – <u>someone gets rich</u>! Today, these changes are happening by the minute and every day people are becoming millionaires by taking advantage of them. You can too!

Creating wealth quickly has almost become a necessity. Because of the world's rapid pace, career cycles have shortened.

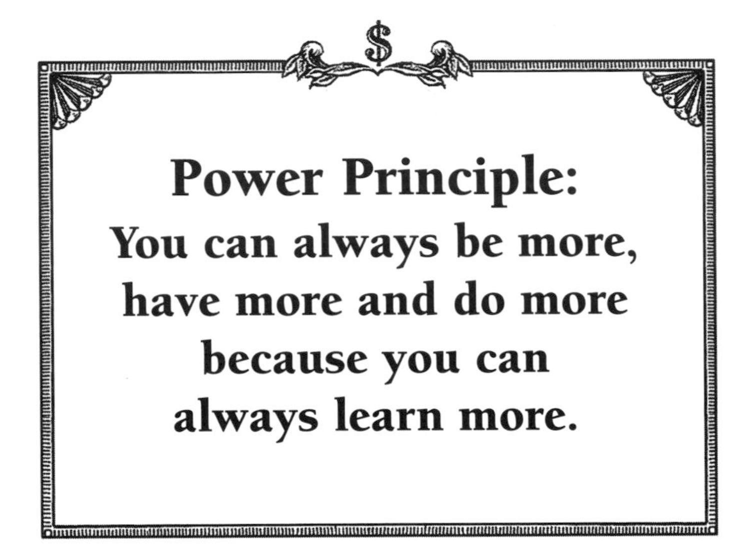
$
Power Principle:
You can always be more,
have more and do more
because you can
always learn more.

Just two decades ago, most people had a "cradle to coffin" mentality; jobs and businesses were a lifetime commitment. But, today, there is no such thing as job or business security.

The current reality is that most of us will go through six or seven complete career or business changes in our lifetime; the average length of each being about five years. Meaning, you "make your money" in that period or you don't make it at all.

Product cycles have also changed: The stages of START - GROWTH - MATURATION - SATURATION - DECLINE, used to take twenty years. Now your product or business could become a dinosaur in five years or less!

Develop a new computer software program and see how long it takes before someone knocks it off or improves it. If you get six months, you're lucky! Look at publishing. Today, if you write a bestseller, how long does it stay on the bestseller list? If you're popular for one whole year, you're almost immortal.

Things have changed. It's time to revise what we deem as a "normal" time frame for success. SpeedWealth is not only possible, it's practical. It's the way of today's high speed world. Either you flow with it or fight against it. The choice is yours. Now for the other question . . .

Is SpeedWealth feasible for <u>you</u>?

What would you do if you wanted to become a professional tennis player or world-class artist? Wouldn't you learn the skill and then practice? In a similar way, you can LEARN to play the game of business . . . and win! Let me repeat, success is a learnable skill. That's why the past does not equal the future.

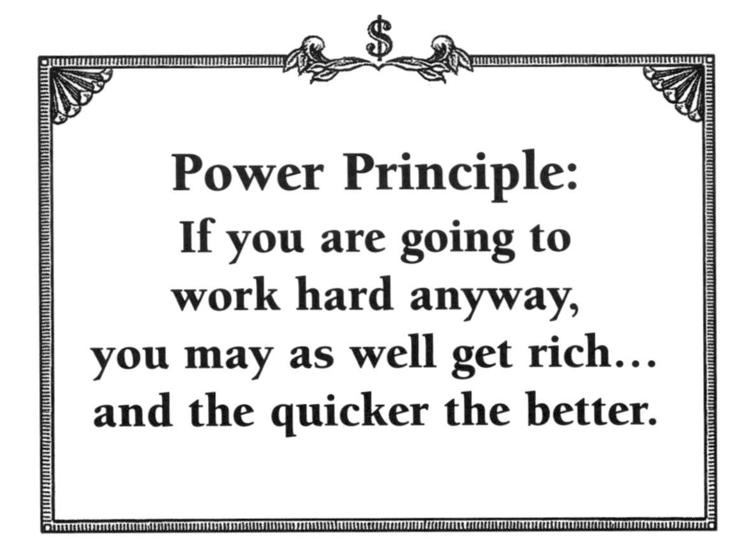
Power Principle:
If you are going to
work hard anyway,
you may as well get rich…
and the quicker the better.

You can always be more, have more
and do more because you can always learn more.

It doesn't matter if you've gone "belly up" three times or have never had a business in your life. The only question is: "Are you WILLING TO LEARN?" If you master the SpeedWealth system and use it, you will get rich in short order.

Another factor to consider is your PERSONALITY. For many of us, attempting to create wealth quickly is more natural. In business, as in racing, there are SPRINTERS, and there are MARATHONERS. Which are you? Some folks are "idea" people. They like to create concepts, start things, grow quickly, and then move on to the next project. Others prefer long-term stability and routine in their work. Until recently, "sprinters," those of us who like to make things happen fast, were considered unstable, almost "flaky." You know the guilt-trip: "What do you mean you want to try something new? You only got into this twelve years ago!!" In today's marketplace, that attitude is archaic. The point is, if you're a sprinter or would be open to trying it — sprint!

The final factor in determining if SpeedWealth is feasible for you is the strength of your DESIRE. You must truly want to create financial freedom fast. Why? Because this isn't going to be a scenic stroll in the park. It's going to be a challenge; a 3 to 5 year mission that will require focus, commitment, and sometimes hard work, at least during the initial stage. But most people already work hard. So my philosophy is simple.

If you are going to work hard anyway,
you might as well get rich . . .
and the quicker the better.

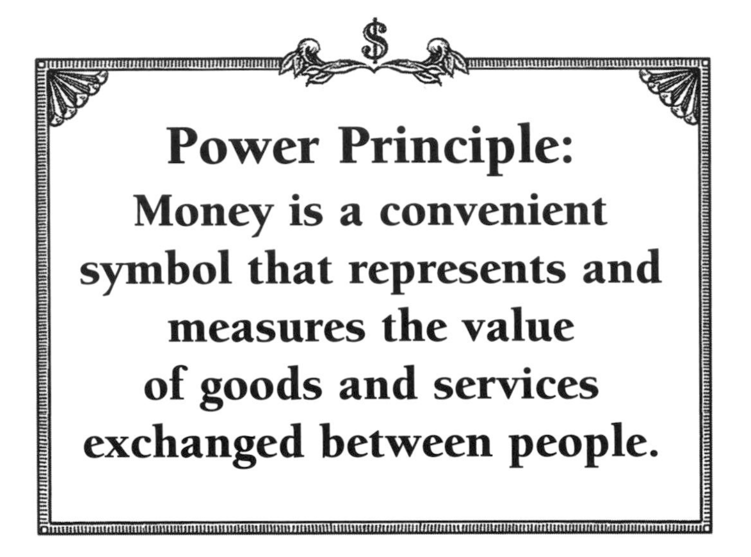
Power Principle:
Money is a convenient symbol that represents and measures the value of goods and services exchanged between people.

SPEEDWEALTH PRINCIPLE #2: DELIVER MASSIVE VALUE

"Money," like it or not, is a huge part of our lives. Unfortunately most people don't really understand it. So what is money anyway?

Money is a convenient symbol that represents and measures the value of goods and services exchanged between people.

The key word in that definition is VALUE. It's value that determines your income.

The Law of Income:
You will be paid in direct proportion to the value you deliver according to the marketplace.

I don't mean to be critical, but I have to tell it like it is: The reason most people are broke is that they don't deliver a lot of VALUE in the eyes of the current marketplace. The important element here is DELIVER.

Many people have good ideas, good intentions, even produce good products or services, but either their value is not considered very valuable in today's marketplace, or they just don't deliver enough of it. It's simple . . .

If you don't deliver a lot, you don't get paid a lot.

So what determines your value in the marketplace?

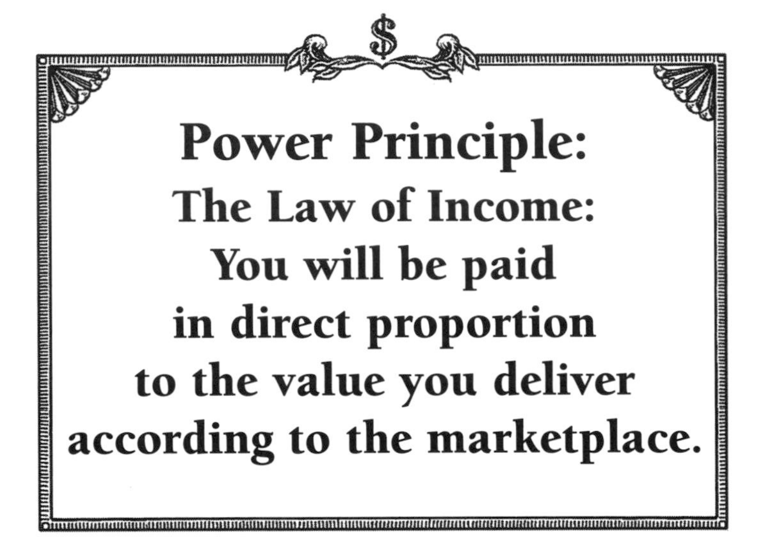
Power Principle:
The Law of Income:
You will be paid
in direct proportion
to the value you deliver
according to the marketplace.

There are four income factors that determine almost to the penny how much you will earn:

Demand + Supply + Quality + Quantity
= $$$

1. The DEMAND for your "value" means how much the marketplace wants it. To create SpeedWealth, you must offer a hot product or service which is in high demand.

When I first started Fitnessland, people tried to buy equipment while I was still renovating the space before the store opened. Within three weeks of opening, customers were lining up outside the door. I made $11,000 net profit on my sixth Saturday . . . because my value was in high demand!

2. The SUPPLY of your "value" reflects how much the marketplace already has of your product or service, and how readily available it is elsewhere.

Why does a brain surgeon earn as much in one day as a gas station attendant earns in a whole year? Because he or she has a rare and specialized skill that is critical when needed. Put bluntly, there are millions who can pump gas, but few who can fix brains.

When supply is limited, value increases.

Think of real estate. Ocean-front property is rare and extremely limited, therefore it is higher in value than property inland. To increase your value in business, you must provide something few others have, or do something in a way that no one else does.

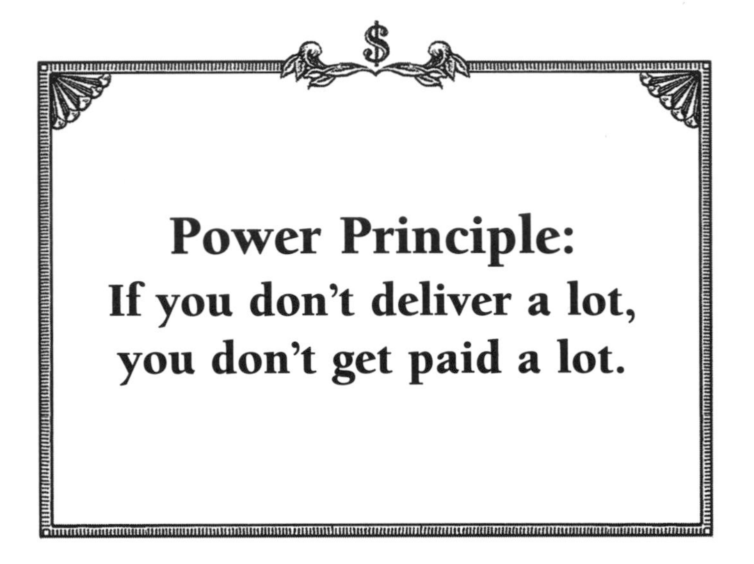
$
Power Principle:
If you don't deliver a lot,
you don't get paid a lot.

3. The QUALITY of your "value" means how good your products and services are — and just as important — how good you are at your business.

The higher the quality, in relation to the price;
the higher the value.

I have a motto in business, "Do it well or don't do it at all. Make it great or don't make it at all."

Does quality affect your income? You bet it does. Do you return to a business if you receive shoddy products or lousy service? Of course not and neither does anyone else!

As for the second part of the quality equation, "how good are you at your business?" The rule is simple.

If you want to get paid the best, be the best!

Keep learning. Study business, study your specific field and study the SpeedWealth principles as if your life depended on it. Financially, it does!

4. The QUANTITY of your "value" is how much of your product or service you deliver.

Of all four factors, most people have the greatest challenge with this one. You may have an excellent product or service and you may even deliver it to the marketplace, but not in enough quantity to create wealth, especially SpeedWealth!

If you want to get paid,
you must deliver your value to people.

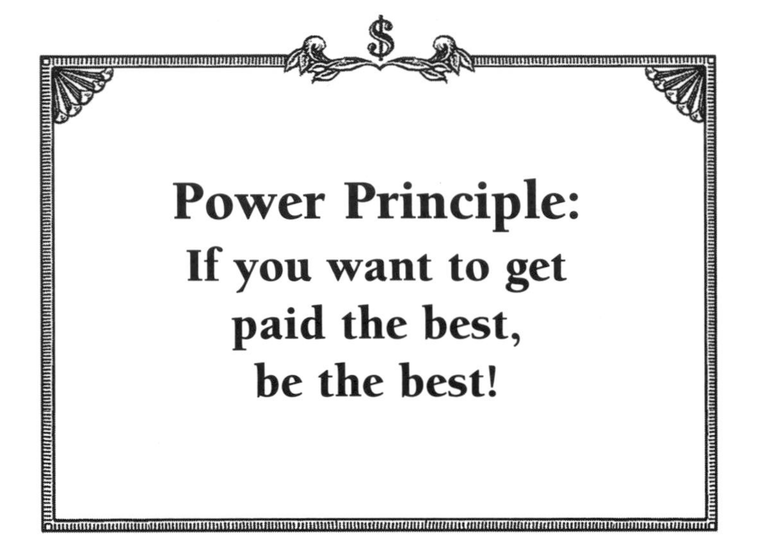
$
Power Principle:
If you want to get
paid the best,
be the best!

If you want to get <u>rich</u>,
You must deliver your value to <u>a lot</u> of people!

That's why . . .

Regardless of the business you're in, part of your revenue should come from product sales.

A product enhances your ability to deliver massive quantities. When you have a product to sell, there are no limits on how much you can produce and deliver, therefore, NO CEILING ON YOUR INCOME.

If you're in a job or service business, and you personally have to perform the service, such as giving massages, there is a definite ceiling on your income. Let's face it, there are only so many massages a masseuse can give in a day! The same limitations hold true if you are a counselor, a consultant, a professional, or anyone else working by the hour or on a salary.

If you do have a personal service business, here are three ways to break through the ceiling on your income. The first is to OFFER A PRODUCT.

It's best if it's an ADD-ON product — one that aligns with your current business, and would benefit your current clients. You can create your own product, or even offer someone else's product you endorse. For example, a masseuse could offer products that benefit the health and well-being of the body, such as nutritional supplements, body oils, aromatherapy products, books on massage and yoga, and relaxation tapes.

A second way is to "CLONE" yourself. The idea is to train or hire others to work for you. Instead of being a sole

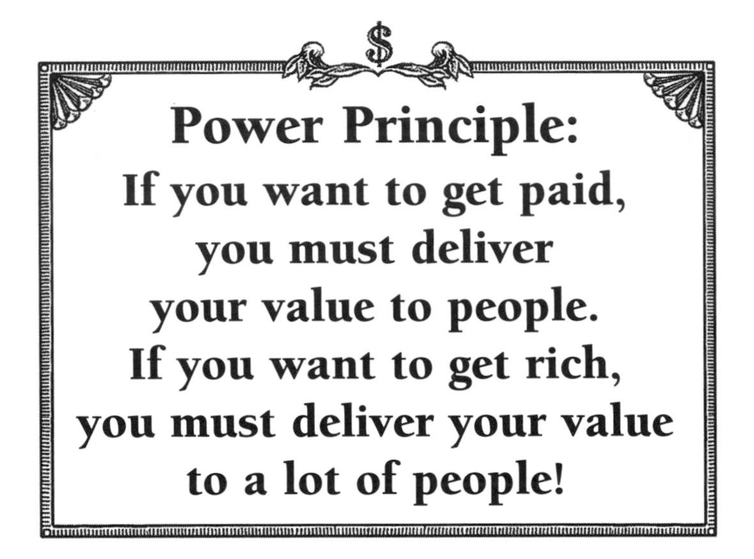

Power Principle:

**If you want to get paid,
you must deliver
your value to people.
If you want to get rich,
you must deliver your value
to a lot of people!**

consultant, you own a consulting company with five, ten, or fifty consultants working for you! This is simply a way of delivering more of your value to the market, which results in more income.

If neither of the above choices are viable and you are adamant about staying in a personal service business or a job, you will probably need a SECOND SOURCE OF INCOME, preferably one that has the "potential" to create wealth. Today there are dozens of "distributor" type opportunities where you can start part-time and move to full-time when your income warrants it. The trick is to choose the right opportunity, and that's the subject of our next principle.

Demand, supply, quality and quantity are the cornerstones of value and delivering massive value is an essential part of the SpeedWealth system. In fact, demand and supply affect the next SpeedWealth principle dramatically . . .

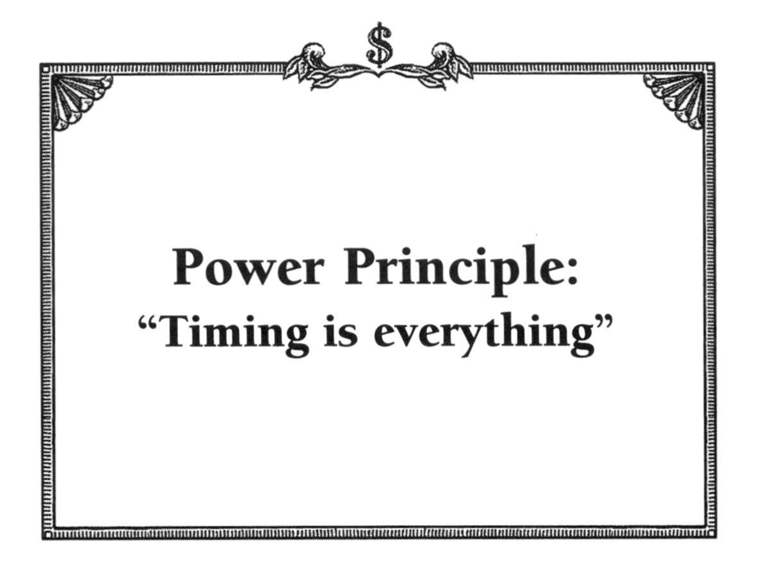
Power Principle:
"Timing is everything"

SPEEDWEALTH PRINCIPLE #3: TIMING: CHOOSE THE RIGHT BUSINESS AT THE RIGHT TIME

Have you heard the saying, "Timing is everything"? That statement is gospel when it comes to making money fast in business. What exactly is timing? It's simply matching your product or service to the wants and needs of the current marketplace – choosing the RIGHT PRODUCT OR SERVICE, in the RIGHT PLACE, at the RIGHT TIME.

This is critical. If you get this step right, you're 50% there! Business ideas and opportunities are like cars. There are 220 m.p.h., Formula-1 race cars; there are decrepit, broken-down jalopies, and every kind of vehicle in between.

The question is, what are you trying to create your fortune with? A race car or a jalopy? If you don't have a concept or at least one product or service that's super hot right now, you need to find one . . . if you want a chance to create wealth quickly!

I'm not necessarily advocating that you change businesses, but if your present concept, product, or service was in a horse race, would the marketplace see it as a thoroughbred or a donkey?

The truth is, almost anyone could have made a "killing" in the home fitness equipment business at the time I did. Why? Because I was riding a super hot trend — a "thoroughbred." The timing was perfect for both the concept and the product.

Choosing the right vehicle at the right time is
a rare and highly profitable skill that can be learned!

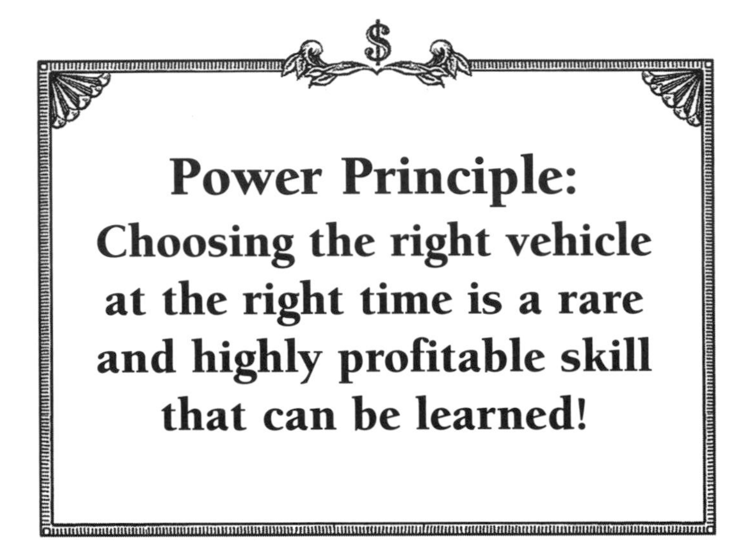
$
Power Principle:
Choosing the right vehicle
at the right time is a rare
and highly profitable skill
that can be learned!

Unfortunately, most people hop on a trend when it's already too late, and the big fortunes have already been made.

On the other hand, being too early is no better. If I had opened Fitnessland three years earlier than I did, I assure you, it would have died. The market wasn't ready — there weren't enough headlines about fitness or enough high-quality, home fitness products available yet. Not enough people were tired of driving to crowded gyms.

You have to learn how to gauge and time the market.
You have to know when to get in,
and when to get out!

In the SpeedWealth system, your intention must be to get in on a "ground-floor opportunity," meaning DEMAND is high and SUPPLY is low. At this time the elevator of opportunity is going up. Time to get on! Later, SUPPLY overtakes DEMAND and the elevator of opportunity starts going down. Time to get off!

Want an example of a ground-floor opportunity available right now? An obvious one is supplying products and services to Internet users. The Internet is a computer communications network that is growing by millions of users a month. It will be as big a medium, if not bigger, than television. What's it all mean? It means as a SpeedWealth entrepreneur, you ACT NOW!

Just like 22-year-old Marc Andreessen did. Working in a college computer lab, he developed a new software program called "Navigator," that made it easier to explore the Internet. In two years, his net worth went from zero to $50 million! "Navigator" was perfectly timed.

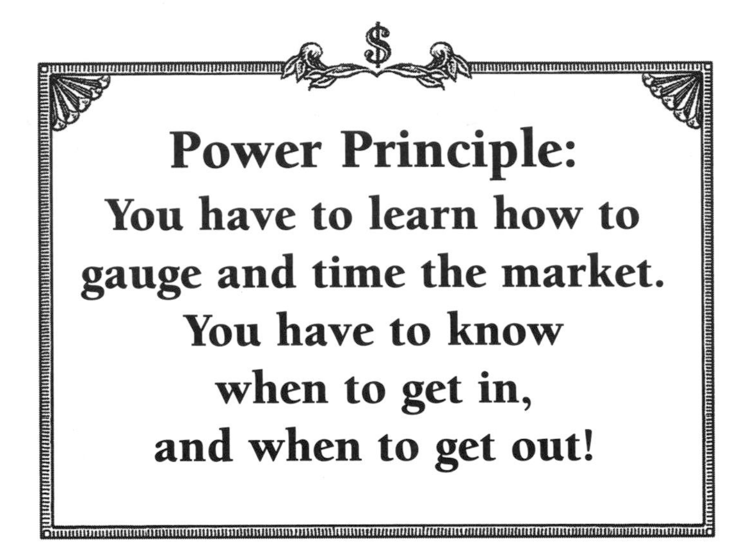

Power Principle:

You have to learn how to gauge and time the market. You have to know when to get in, and when to get out!

Today's hottest opportunities are not just in high-tech industries. One of the most popular, eye-opening sessions I teach at my SpeedWealth Bootcamp is called, "How to Generate Million Dollar Opportunities Every 60 Seconds." Let me share a couple of these strategies with you.

One fast and easy way to get rich is to . . .

Model a proven winner.

In other words, copy someone who is making a mint right now.

You want to employ a principle called "Lag Time," which is the time it takes for a hot idea to spread from one geographical region to another. For instance, customers can be lining up for a hot new product or concept in Los Angeles that has not even been heard of yet in Atlanta. Right now there are dozens of entrepreneurs making a fortune with ground-floor opportunities that have not yet been exposed in other parts of the country. Find one of these new concepts and do the same thing, or IMPROVE ON IT, in your geographic area! Use the original as a proven blueprint to success.

Right now, coffeehouses are super hot in some areas of the country, but other spots are still virgin territories. That means if you're broke in saturated Seattle, you can always go to "wide open" Omaha and get rich.

Another simple but incredibly fast way to make a fortune is called the PIGGYBACK technique. Instead of copying someone else, you AFFILIATE with someone or something that's already a winner. You know the old saying . . .

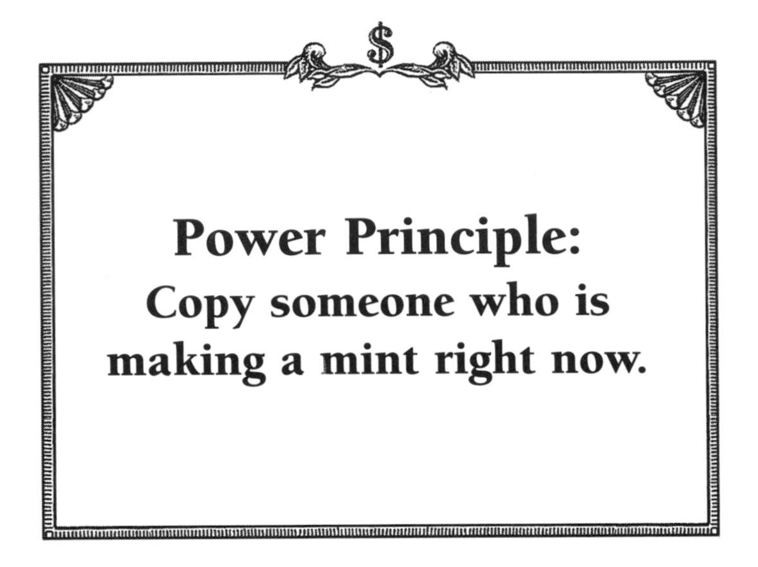
Power Principle:
Copy someone who is
making a mint right now.

"If you can't beat 'em, join 'em!"

It's often faster and easier to affiliate with a company that's up and running rather than to start from scratch. Why reinvent the wheel? They may have exclusive products or a major distribution network in place, rare technology, or expensive production facilities already established.

I have an acquaintance who found a particularly good engine additive that was selling like "hot cakes" in the U.S., but the manufacturer wasn't marketing it anywhere else.

He was clever. He paid $1,000 for the option to buy the international rights for $100,000, payable in 6 months. Then he placed classified ads in dozens of newspapers and trade journals, worldwide, offering the exclusive distribution rights for specific territories. In only four months he sold 80 regions at $25,000 each, making $2 million up-front, plus five cents on every can! Best of all, he never touched the product. He set it up so the new distributors dealt directly with the manufacturer. Do you know what he's doing now? NOTHING!

As a SpeedWealth entrepreneur, you want to . . .

Take advantage of the new "global economy."

There are thousands of popular American products that are not marketed across any borders and thousands of popular international products that are not marketed in the U.S. These are all dynamite opportunities!

Anyone, and I do mean anyone, can become rich quickly using the Piggyback technique. It's one of my favorites because

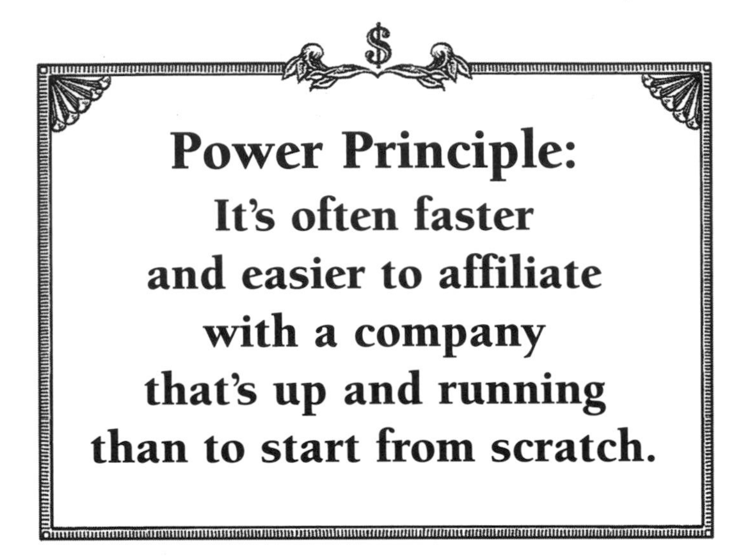
Power Principle:
It's often faster
and easier to affiliate
with a company
that's up and running
than to start from scratch.

you're like a jockey; you find the best horse on the track, hop on, and ride it to the winner's circle!

Along the same lines, another surefire SpeedWealth tactic is called remarketing "UNDER-MARKETED" products and services. Have you ever seen or used a product that you think is fantastic, works like a miracle, but hardly anyone else knows about it? These are what I call "under-marketed" products. Did you know there are 71 different ways to market and distribute a product or service? Most companies only use 2 or 3 methods at best. Meanwhile, you can often get the rights to promote their product through dozens of other channels and to different market niches.

Can you think of an easier way to "get rich quick" than to have the rights to a "miracle product" and then market the heck out of it? It's a dream come true. Of course, you'll want to become a master at marketing, but again, this skill can be learned.

Remember, timing is everything. If you choose the right product at the right time, your road to SpeedWealth will be decidedly faster and easier!

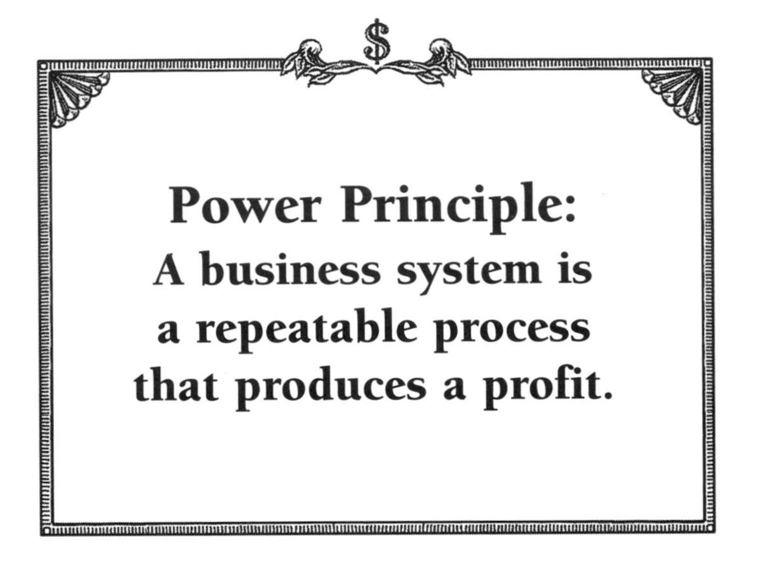

Power Principle:
A business system is a repeatable process that produces a profit.

SPEEDWEALTH PRINCIPLE #4:
SYSTEMIZE

What happens if you try to build a house on a weak foundation? The house eventually cracks or caves in. That's why before you can build a big house, you must build a solid foundation. The business equivalent to building a solid foundation is called "CREATING A SYSTEM."

Since the word "system" is a generic term, let me define what it means for business purposes . . .

A business system is a "repeatable process
that produces a profit."

The idea is to systemize your business so that you can effectively and efficiently sell and support your product or service in larger quantities as you grow. What if a tree grows tall without firm roots? All may be well when things are calm, but with the first big wind storm, it topples over and dies. It's the same in business. If you try to expand but have no effective system in place, the business is doomed. I call this the "Expansion Dilemma." You've probably heard of businesses going well until they tried to expand. Then all of a sudden they're in trouble. Now you understand why. They grew beyond their effective means of support, their roots, their foundation and their system (if they had one at all).

So how do you create an effective business system? For now, let me share rule number one: "Keep it simple." I have a philosophy that . . .

Business is simple.
People are complicated.

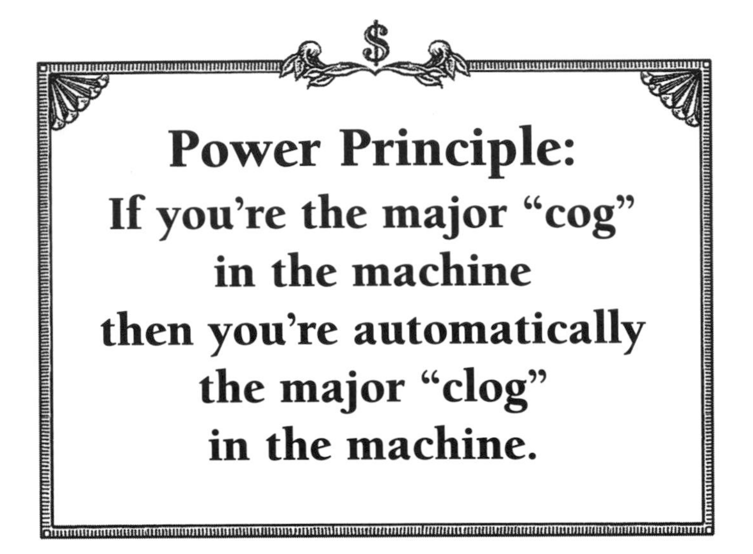
$
Power Principle:
If you're the major "cog"
in the machine
then you're automatically
the major "clog"
in the machine.

Any business should consist of only three parts:

Marketing; Production; Administration.

You must design specific "processes" for each of these three areas so they run smoothly, almost automatically. The idea is to create a business that works like a well-oiled machine — a MONEY MACHINE!

Your system must be organized, it must produce a profit, and it must support rapid growth. Finally, and this is essential if you want to create wealth quickly, your system must be a repeatable process that CAN WORK WITHOUT YOU! Why? Because as we discussed earlier, in order to create wealth you cannot have a ceiling on your income. Your earnings must be unlimited.

If you're the major "cog" in the machine
then you're automatically
the major "clog" in the machine.

If you have to be physically present for your business to work, it can only grow to the extent that you can personally handle. It doesn't matter how brilliant and energetic you are, you still only have 24 hours in a day! And besides, what good is creating wealth if you're going to kill yourself in the process?

A SpeedWealth entrepreneur is a co-ordinator.
He or she is the conductor of the orchestra.

Even though the conductor may be a master at playing an instrument, they don't, because if they did, no one would be leading the orchestra. It can be quite a challenge for a small-business owner to "conduct the orchestra" on a full-time basis,

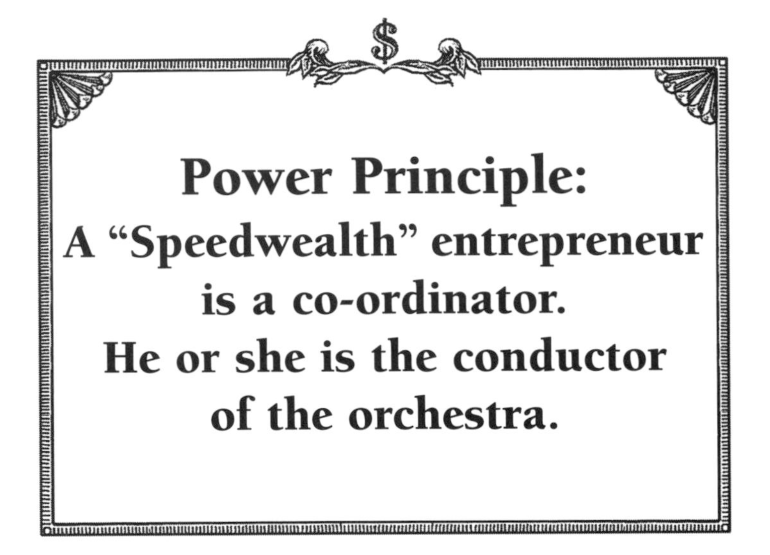
$
Power Principle:
A "Speedwealth" entrepreneur
is a co-ordinator.
He or she is the conductor
of the orchestra.

but this position is absolutely necessary if you're serious about creating wealth quickly.

Notice every large corporation has a president or CEO whose sole position is to hold the vision, co-ordinate all the parts, develop opportunities for growth, and search for ways to increase profits. It becomes a chicken-and-egg question. Was the position created because the corporation grew, or did the corporation grow because they created this position? My bet is the latter. I'm not saying you can't continue to do all the other tasks, just keep in mind what I said, "Everywhere you are a cog, eventually, as you grow, you will become a clog." Your primary responsibility is to . . .

Work on the business, instead of in the business.

One of the most important elements of the SpeedWealth system is that your business cannot be dependent or limited by any one person, especially YOU. This will become critical during the final step of the program.

I highly recommend a book called *The E-Myth*, by Michael Gerber. In it, he suggests you build your business as if it were going to become a successful franchise organization, even if you have no intention to franchise. Imagine your business will be the prototype for one hundred more locations or that your sales process is going to be repeated 10,000 times — both WITHOUT your direct involvement!

For the first six months at Fitnessland, I hardly stepped foot outside the store, while I set up the system, knocked out the kinks, and created a business "model" that worked. After that, I hardly stepped foot inside the store. I trained someone else to manage the day-to-day operations, while I concentrated on growth.

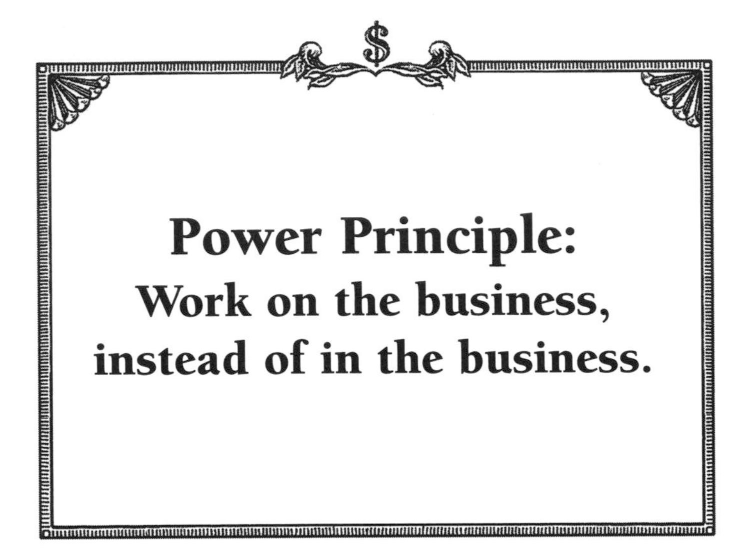
$
Power Principle:
Work on the business,
instead of in the business.

Realize that . . .

The system gives you freedom.

First, in terms of TIME. With a system, you get to relax, play, and be with your loved ones, all while your business is running, growing, and producing big profits! Having an effective system working "instead" of you, is vital to "enjoying the journey."

Second, in terms of MONEY. With a strong system in place, you will have two options. One, you'll be able to hand over the reins of authority and have an excellent passive income while you golf, ski, meditate, or do whatever else you like. Two, you can "cash out" and become an instant millionaire.

In any of these cases, because you created a "system," you win!

O.K., let's assume you've done your testing, you've worked out the kinks, and you now have a money machine — a single success, a single pilot or a single sales method that systematically produces a profit without you. What do you do next?

The answer is . . .

"If it works, keep doing it."

You do it again, and again, and again.

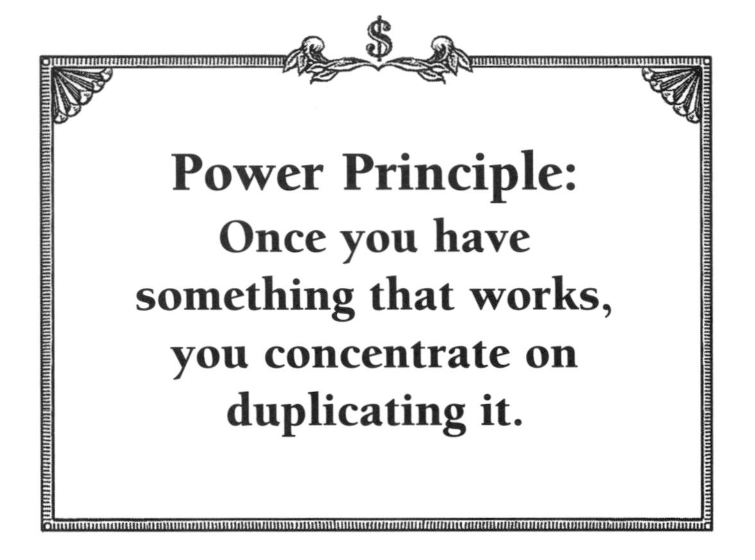

Power Principle:
Once you have something that works, you concentrate on duplicating it.

SPEEDWEALTH PRINCIPLE #5: DUPLICATE

Once you have "something" that works, you concentrate on DUPLICATING it. This is why creating a system that's organized to deliver and support large quantities of your value, without your presence, is so vital. It allows for duplication.

Your completed system is the model or "COOKIE CUTTER," you use to duplicate your success over and over again. First you create something that works well on a small scale, maybe one store, one office, or a sale to one person. Then you repeat the process, again and again. It's that simple!

The SpeedWealth entrepreneur understands that if you can make a profit on one location, the question is, how many similar locations can you create? If you can make a profit on one transaction, the question is, how many similar transactions can you make? The key question is . . .

"How do I get my product or service
into the hands of the largest numbers of people?"

Duplication is simply a way of increasing the quantity of the value you deliver. And when you increase your quantity, you increase your income!

More people have created wealth using the "cookie cutter" approach than any other method in history. Have you heard of a gentleman named Sam Walton? His little empire is called WAL-MART. Sam started with one small store, in one small town, that produced one small profit. Then he systemized the store so that it worked efficiently without him. This became the cookie cutter he used to roll out 1,500 "cookies," otherwise

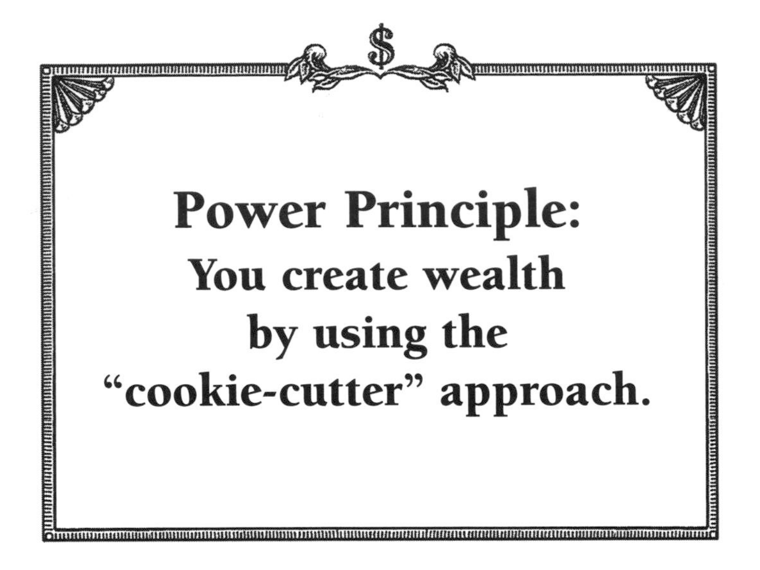
$
Power Principle:
You create wealth
by using the
“cookie-cutter” approach.

known as Wal-Mart stores, in hundreds of small towns across America.

Sam Walton was a true master of the SpeedWealth system. He died a few years ago as one of the richest people on the planet, amassing a personal net worth of over $7 billion dollars. That's billion, with a capital "B."

Everyone knows McDonald's. Back in the '50's, Ray Kroc uncovered a "sizzling" hot concept: fast food, burgers, fries and shakes. Then he systemized his marketing, production, and operations so that this one store worked efficiently and profitably. He then duplicated by allowing others to use his profitable system. This method of expansion is now known as franchising. Today, there are thousands of McDonald's outlets around the world selling to millions of people daily. Ray Kroc was another master of the SpeedWealth system who applied the power of DUPLICATION. Before he died, Ray Kroc amassed a net worth of over $4 billion. That's <u>another</u> capital "B."

Have you heard of Amway, Mary Kay, Herbalife, or NuSkin? They are all network or multi-level marketing companies. This is simply another form of DUPLICATION. You use the product, then refer it to someone else, who does the same thing and on and on and on. In fact, the entire network marketing process is based on the SpeedWealth principles. Timing, systemization and duplication are inherent and already built into the multi-level methodology.

The best network marketers understand that duplication can make you rich! These network marketing distributors have "downlines" numbering over 20,000 people, and generate incomes of over $1,000,000 a <u>year</u>!

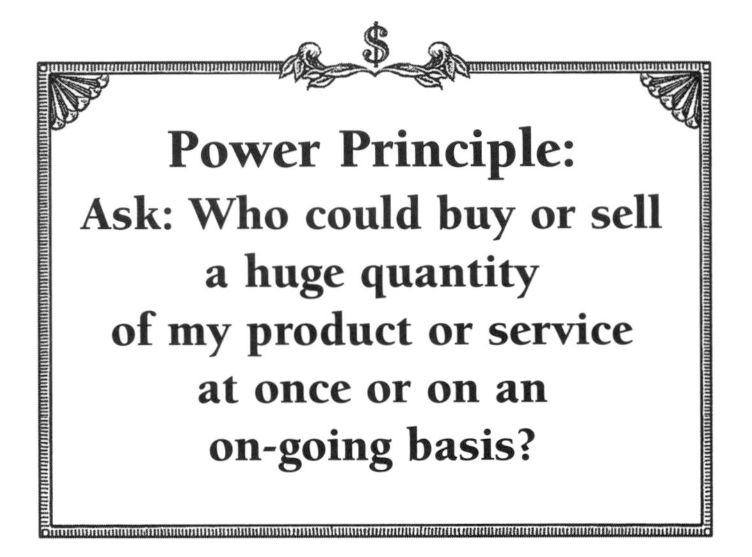
Power Principle:
Ask: Who could buy or sell
a huge quantity
of my product or service
at once or on an
on-going basis?

Remember, the idea behind duplication is getting your value distributed to as many people as possible, as quickly as possible. This is where a lot of business owners run into trouble. They can't seem to get exposure. They don't have the funds for heavy advertising campaigns and they're not adept at marketing. What can they do?

One SpeedWealth strategy is to find buyers who can purchase or sell large volumes of your products or services. The question you always want to ask is . . .

Who could buy or sell a huge quantity
of my product or service
at once or on an on-going basis?

It brings to mind a student who attended one of my business "bootcamps." He had created a "How to Paint Your House" video, and was trying to sell these videos to small retail outlets.

After the session I mentioned earlier, "71 Ways to Market and Distribute Your Product," he went out into the hall, used the phone, and came back with a huge smile on his face. With a single call, he sold his video to one of the largest paint manufacturers in the world!! The video would be used as a "premium" and given away free with each purchase of five or more gallons of paint. His first order was for 100,000 units, and my student's profit was about $1 on each.

As you can see, making money is easy once you understand duplication.

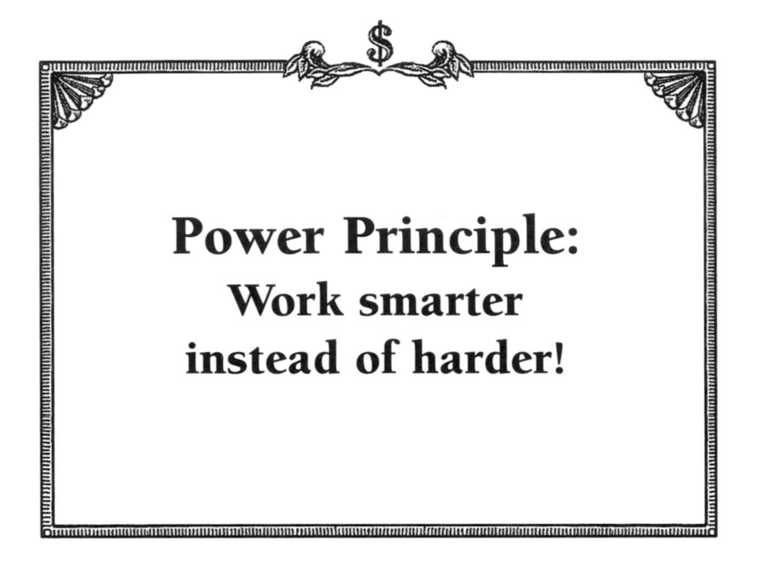
$
Power Principle:
Work smarter
instead of harder!

SPEEDWEALTH PRINCIPLE #6: LEVERAGE

LEVERAGE means doing MORE with LESS. It's not so much a "what" you do, but rather a "how" you do it. Leverage uses specific tactics and strategies that allow you to . . .

Work smarter instead of harder!

One of my business mottos is . . .

"If you're not using leverage,
you're working too hard, and earning too little!"

Leverage starts with replacing yourself or much of what you do personally.

As a SpeedWealth practitioner you want to constantly be asking yourself . . .

"How can I provide people with my value,
my products or services, while I sleep?"

When you can answer this question and execute the answer, you've got it made.

Have you heard of Tony Robbins? He is a master speaker and author. By his own account, he held over 200 seminars in a single year and yet barely broke even. He finally decided to tape his information and sell his program via 30-minute TV "infomercials." This is a perfect example of leverage. By putting his PRODUCT on TV, he was able to reach a lot more people and make a lot more money with a lot less time, travel and personal effort.

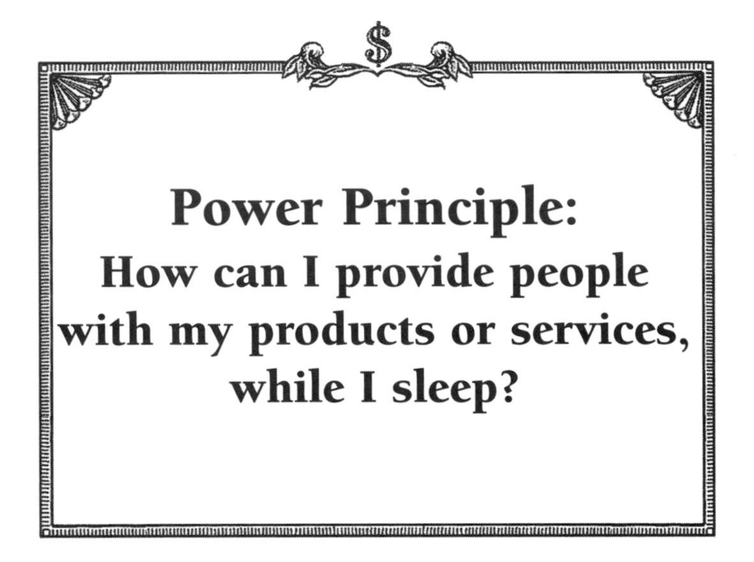

Power Principle:
How can I provide people with my products or services, while I sleep?

Now he's employing leverage even further. Tony now hosts a single LIVE seminar and then "simulcasts" it via satellite to hundreds of movie theaters all over the country. Using high technology, audiences get to interact in the actual course. Like alchemy, his audience of 300 is transformed into 30,000!

Tony Robbins is extremely successful. Partly due to his valuable information, but mostly because he is a master of the SpeedWealth system and constantly searches for ways to increase his leverage.

Let's look at another form of leverage. Remember the student I told you about with the "Paint Your House" video? Remember how he got an opening order for 100,000 units? Well, the story's not over. The next session of the bootcamp was about creating SpeedWealth through "licensing." Once again he went out at the next break and made a phone call. This time, he came back with an even bigger smile. He had changed the arrangement with the paint manufacturer. Instead of SELLING the videos to them, he LICENSED them the rights to duplicate the video themselves. They immediately upped their initial run to 250,000 units. Why? Because they could now choose their own suppliers, giving them full control of product quality and lowering their costs.

Licensing is an extremely-high form of leverage. My student was able to sell more with less of his own time and money. And since his royalty percentage remained the same, his income skyrocketed.

By the way, what did he do with all the extra time on his hands? He utilized another form of leverage; ADD-ON and REPEAT SALES, and immediately began creating Volume 2 of

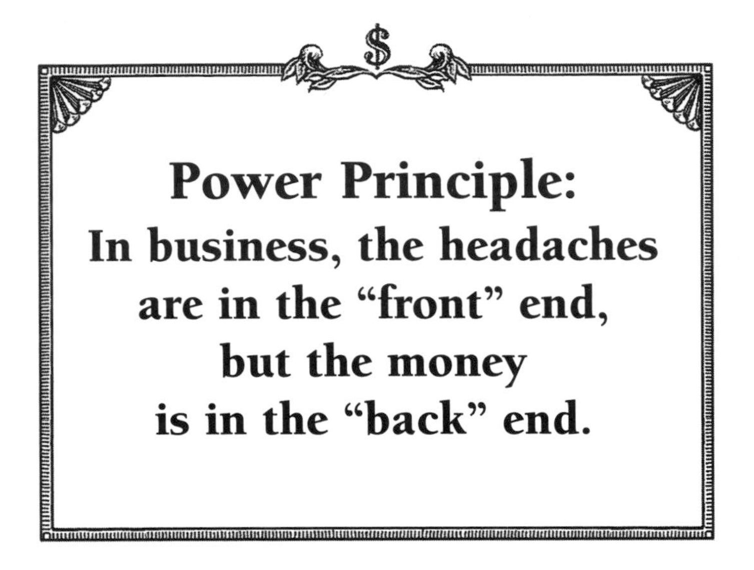
$
Power Principle:
In business, the headaches
are in the "front" end,
but the money
is in the "back" end.

his "house painting" video "SERIES," covering specialty areas like decks, raingutters, and outside doors.

One of the most powerful ways to leverage is to fully utilize your database. Supporting your customers with additional products and services, giving them reasons to return again and again produces extremely high profits because you've already paid the high cost of getting the customer the first time. These are called "back end" sales and that's why I say . . .

"In business, the headaches are in the front end,
but the money's in the back end."

Yet another exciting form of leverage is PARTNERSHIP MARKETING, or JOINT VENTURING. Consider the example of *USA Today's* 900# Sports Line. Do you think that *USA Today* is in the 900# business? No way! They partner with an outside company, who operates the lines while *USA Today* does the advertising; a synergistic relationship that allows each company to use its strengths. That's why "partnership" marketing is popular today and will become even more popular in the future. In fact, a great ground-floor opportunity available right now is starting a "partnership marketing" agency. You would match companies who could work together, and receive a percentage of the resulting services.

Leverage is a massive subject. If you want more details, we get into it heavily in our SpeedWealth Bootcamp and in our tape programs. For now however, let me share a few more quick examples of leverage with you:

- Leverage is starting your business with little or none of your own money.

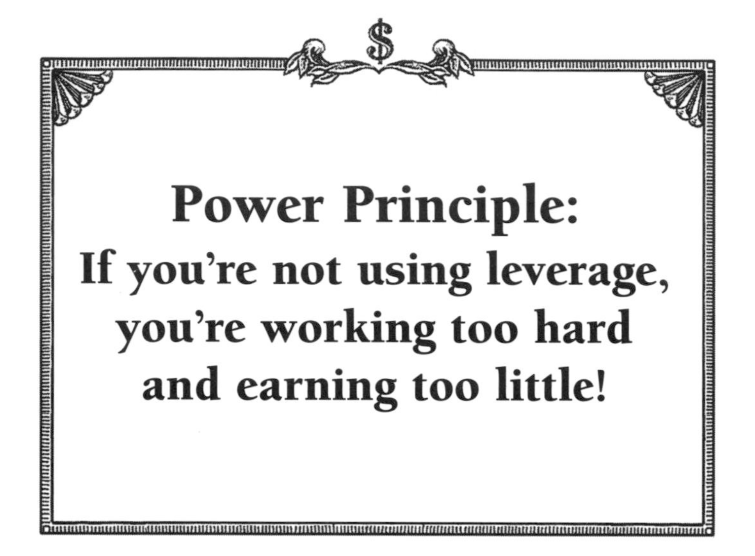
Power Principle:
If you're not using leverage,
you're working too hard
and earning too little!

- Leverage is using other people's talents, skills, contacts, credibility, and resources.
- Leverage is fully utilizing the latest technologies in computers, software and telecommunications to increase your speed and efficiency.
- Leverage is using the power of the media to get millions of dollars of free publicity.
- Leverage is borrowing celebrity fame for endorsements.
- Leverage is selling products before you have them, or at least, before you have to pay for them!
- Leverage is expanding your business using your customer's or supplier's money.
- Leverage is getting the best people in your industry to work for you now, for almost "nothing."
- Leverage is getting more from each of your employees by properly training them, treating them well, and giving them the space to express their true talents.
- Leverage is getting more from yourself, enhancing your business knowledge, developing yourself personally and increasing your stamina and energy.
- Leverage is managing your time more effectively so you do the right things instead of just do things right.
- Leverage is a MINDSET. It's an ART. It's a SCIENCE. It's an essential piece of the SpeedWealth puzzle. It often separates those who create financial freedom quickly, from those who continue to struggle for the rest of their lives. Remember . . .

If you're not using leverage,
you're working too hard and earning too little!

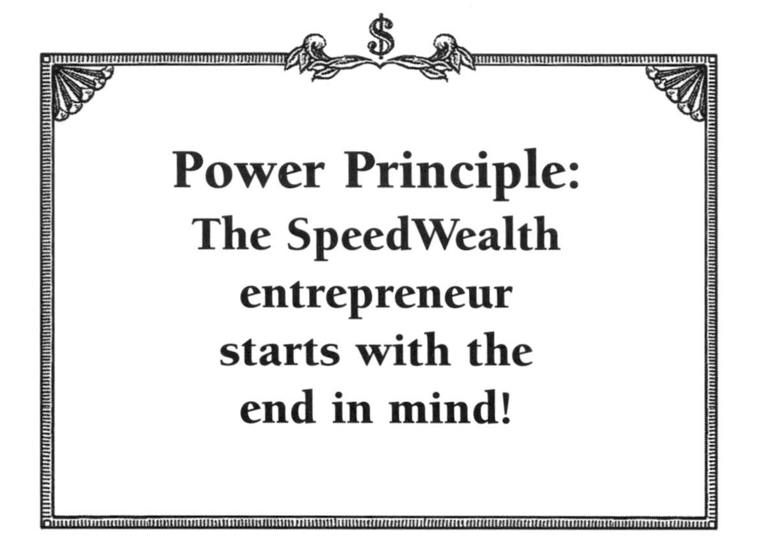
$
Power Principle:
The SpeedWealth
entrepreneur
starts with the
end in mind!

SPEEDWEALTH PRINCIPLE #7: CASHING OUT

This principle is the culmination of all the steps, and ties the entire SpeedWealth system together. One of the primary differences between a SpeedWealth entrepreneur and the average business owner is that they . . .

Start with the end in mind!

By following the SpeedWealth system to the letter, in three to five years, you will have four enviable choices:

1. You can keep the business, continue to work "hands-on," and make a huge INCOME.

OR 2. You can keep the business, and cash out your TIME by delegating the day-to-day affairs, and make a huge PASSIVE INCOME.

OR 3. You can sell all or part of the business and become an INSTANT MILLIONAIRE.

OR 4. You can create a combination of all of the above.

In any case, you've hit the jackpot!

I want to share a little secret . . .

You will never make as much money <u>running</u> a business as <u>selling</u> a business!

The most lucrative product you can ever sell is the business itself. By following the SpeedWealth process, you will have automatically set up your business as an extremely valuable and salable commodity.

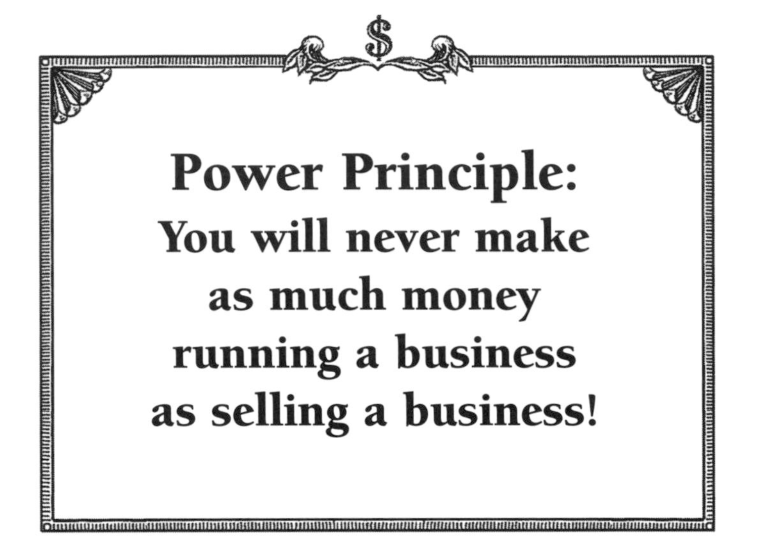

Power Principle:

You will never make as much money running a business as selling a business!

Now do you see why it's so critical that your business be able to run without you? Because when it comes time to sell your business, the better it can run and profit without you as an integral part of the package, the HIGHER THE VALUE AND PRICE!!

Let's face it, if YOU were buying a business, would you want its success to be dependent on any one person — especially the owner, who wants to sell and leave it? Of course not! So what do buyers want? What are they really buying? Primarily three things: profits, the continuation of those profits, and the potential growth of those profits. Buyers want a solid, proven, well-run money machine that churns out a healthy income on an on-going basis and runs without a lot of maintenance.

So, by using the SpeedWealth system, that's exactly what you create – a high-powered money machine that has already been duplicated several times, and still has plenty of room for growth. Once you have accomplished this task, big companies will line up to buy your business for $1, 2, 3 million, or more.

So when in the process do you have to start thinking about all this? At the beginning! In the SpeedWealth system, it's imperative that you think "SELL" from day one . . .

You come in with the intention to cash out!

From the very beginning of Fitnessland, my goal was to build the business, as quickly as possible, to a point where it was worth at least a million after-tax dollars, THEN SELL! And that's exactly what I did! And exactly what you can do too!

People often ask, can you "cash out" if you're a distributor or a "professional" or own a "home" business? The answer is

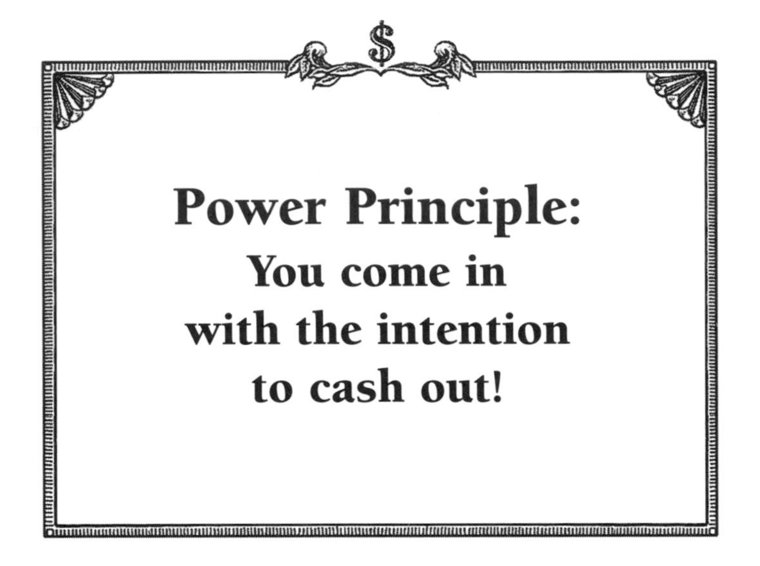

Power Principle:

You come in with the intention to cash out!

contingent on the way you've set up your operation. If you've followed the SpeedWealth program and systemized your business into a money machine that can work without you, and if you've designed it so your customers are happy dealing with the company and its representatives instead of only you personally, then ABSOLUTELY YES! You can sell, and for big, big money.

I know a network marketer who recently sold his "down-line" for mega-bucks, plus an on-going percentage of the purchaser's income! I know of a bill auditor, who sold her "home business" for a small fortune because of her proven marketing system and her extensive client list.

I'm friends with a chiropractor who just cashed out his practice and made a mint. Even though he had a personal service business, he was smart from the start and did not use his "personal" name as his business name. Think about it, would you want someone else's personal name on your new business? Neither would most buyers.

Remember, I'm not saying you have to sell your successful company, but because you've used the SpeedWealth system and set it up to sell from the beginning, you will at least have the choice of becoming an instant millionaire if you want to!

Remember too, you can sell half your shares, like I did, and pocket a very handsome "chunk of change," and perhaps stay on as President or Chairman of the Board!

Another way to cash out a portion of your ownership is by GOING PUBLIC.

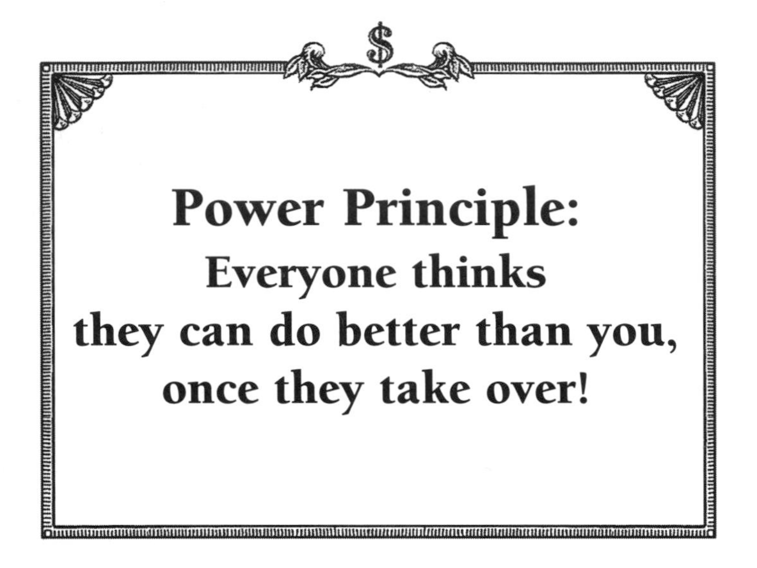

Power Principle:

Everyone thinks they can do better than you, once they take over!

IPO's (initial public offerings) are once again in vogue. The big trend is to start a business, prove its viability in the marketplace, and then go public, using the funds to expand nationally, or even internationally. Meanwhile, you own 2.2 zillion shares, part of which you can cash-in, a few months after the offering!

Today, many businesses are choosing to fund their expansion by going public instead of franchising. The directors always "say" this gives them more control. Maybe. Maybe not. What is certain, however, is that going public gives them a chance to make a quick personal fortune! Look at Navigator's two directors. As I mentioned, in less than two years, Marc Andreessen's shares were worth $50 million. Sounds great until you hear that his partner, Jim Clark's shares became worth $500 MILLION!! This is "SpeedWealth" in all its glory.

Again, when do you consider going public? Preferably right from the beginning. Don't be too quick to rule out this wealth -producing option. It might just be right for you and it's not nearly as difficult as most people think. The key is to find the right person to guide you through it!

Regardless of how you're going to cash out, it's critical to learn the key factors that determine the value of a business for the purpose of selling. This way, you know exactly what areas of the business to focus on and can sell for the most money possible.

Some people would say NET PROFIT is most important, and that's often true, but in my experience, GROSS SALES are just as essential. Why? First, high gross sales show high potential. Second, is "human psychology." The fact is . . .

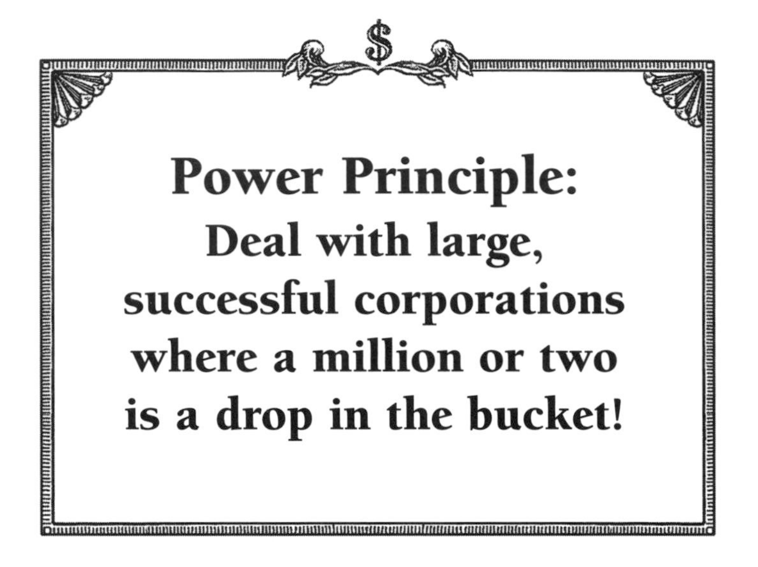
$
Power Principle:
Deal with large,
successful corporations
where a million or two
is a drop in the bucket!

Everyone thinks they can do better than you,
once they take over!

If you've got massive gross sales but minor net profits, most buyers will think you're a "half-wit" who just doesn't know how to run a business. And once they get their expert hands on the control levers, profits will soar through the roof! Once again, maybe — maybe not!

Another key selling factor is, "who is buying your company?" What is the purchaser's wherewithal? In the SpeedWealth system, we deal primarily with major corporations that have full-on acquisition departments and buy businesses on a regular basis. You want to deal only with large, successful corporations that are accustomed to paying top dollar for everything. A company where a million or two is a drop in the bucket! Believe it or not, the $1.6 million Heinz paid for Fitnessland was the "least" they'd ever spent for a business. To them, the deal was a "no brainer" and that's just the way I wanted it!

CASHING OUT, be it by selling all or part of your business, is the crowning jewel of the SpeedWealth system. It's what allowed me to go from zero to a million in only 2 1/2 years, and why I'm confident that if you follow the SpeedWealth system to the letter, in 3 to 5 years, you can be a millionaire too!

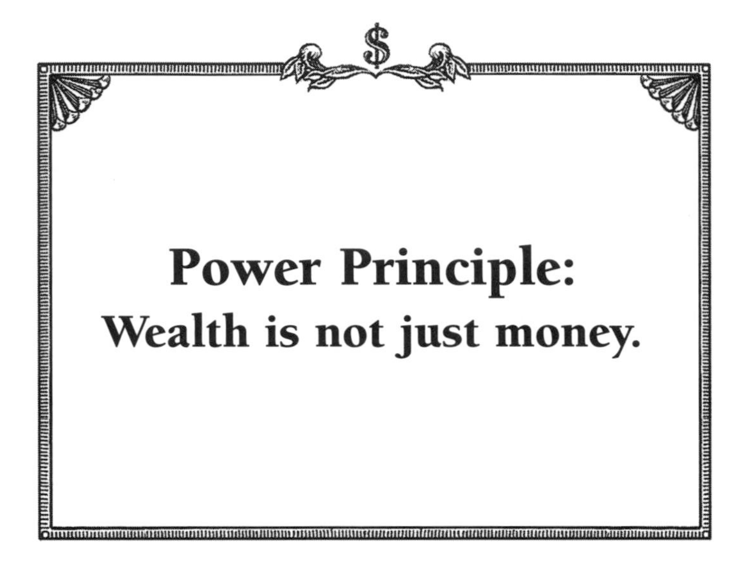
Power Principle:
Wealth is not just money.

ENJOYING YOUR "MISSION TO MILLIONS"

The name of this program is Speed "Wealth," not Speed "Money." The SpeedWealth system is more than just making money, it's the ability to enjoy the journey along the way and grow your business without the usual stress and struggle.

Wealth is not just money. For most people, wealth includes an abundance of money, free time, loving relationships, inner peace, and having a sense of meaning and fulfillment.

Not long ago I had the biggest scare of my life. My doctor told me he thought I had lymphoma. He scheduled me for surgery and did a biopsy on a lump that had developed in my throat. It took four agonizing days for the results to come in. During that wait, my entire life changed. I was really scared, not so much about dying, but about not having fully lived! I knew I hadn't given enough attention to the true priorities in life: my wife, my children, my inner spirit, and just taking time to play. I vowed if I ever got out of this mess, I would change. I'd never take another day for granted and would live each moment recognizing it as the gift it truly is. I vowed that from then on, I wasn't going to let myself become obsessed with results. Instead, I'd relish the journey and achieve my goals with peace and joy instead of stress and struggle.

Finally the pathology report came back. I had a tumor but it was benign, non-malignant. I was going to live.

Today I consider that scare a blessing. It gave me impetus to teach and help others learn lessons that might improve their lives. It's also become the basis for my most important message and the final SpeedWealth principle . . .

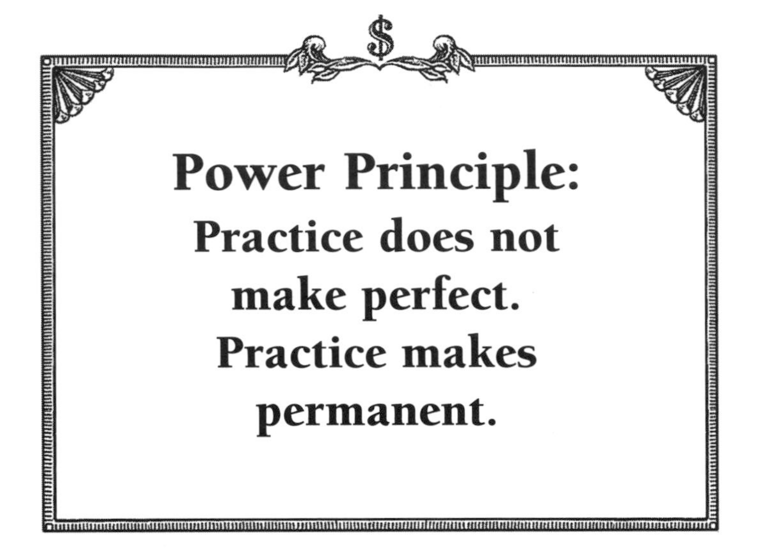
Power Principle:
Practice does not
make perfect.
Practice makes
permanent.

SPEEDWEALTH PRINCIPLE #8: DO IT NOW!

Life is short! Whatever you want to do, do it now. Whatever you want to be, be that now. Whatever you want to have, go for it now! When it comes to the important things in life, don't wait until tomorrow. Tomorrow may not come.

Practice being happy now!

Why do I say "practice"? Because "practice makes perfect," right? Wrong! That's a massive misconception!

Practice does not make perfect.
Practice makes permanent.

People are creatures of HABIT. On a daily basis, if you practice pessimism and struggle, you become very good at it. You become unconsciously competent. Pessimism and struggle become almost automatic to a point where even when you want to change, happiness becomes almost impossible.

The important thing to remember is . . .

One process does not lead to another.

Practicing pitching leads to being a good pitcher, not catcher. Practicing overwhelm leads to overwhelm, not inner peace. And practicing being miserable leads to misery, not happiness.

If you wait until everything is going great before you practice happiness, you may wait a long time. Not because things will never be great, but because you've become a master at being unhappy. Unhappiness will be your habit!

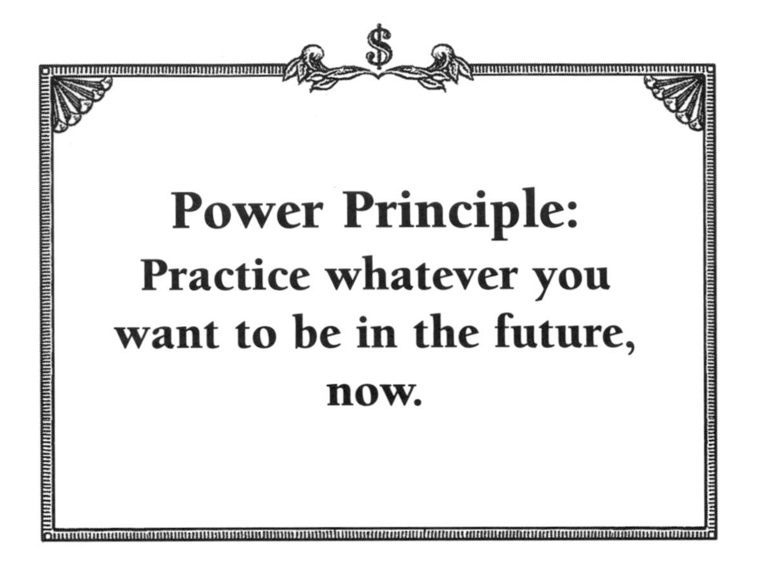
Power Principle:
Practice whatever you want to be in the future, now.

That's why it's critical, no matter what other objectives you're attempting to achieve, you remember to practice happiness RIGHT NOW, in this very moment!

Part of the SpeedWealth strategy is to . . .

Practice whatever you want to be in the future, now.

If you want a life of inner peace, practice being peaceful now. If, one day, you want total confidence, practice being totally confident now. If some day you want to be successful, practice being successful now.

Eventually, these traits become your habits, your natural way of being. You won't have to think about them, you will be them. And your life TODAY, will be what you always wished it would be like, tomorrow.

The key is to enjoy the journey. You want to blend money with meaning, profit with purpose, and "street-smarts" with heart.

Thank goodness, along with the lessons I learned in business, I learned some essential life lessons too. To me, these are the most important messages I share. What is unfortunate however, is that even though most people want to be happy, have more fun, laugh more, love more and enjoy their lives more, it's difficult to concentrate on these things when you're struggling financially.

Money problems can take the luster out of life. I'm not saying money is everything.

Money isn't everything unless you don't have any,
then it seems to become everything.

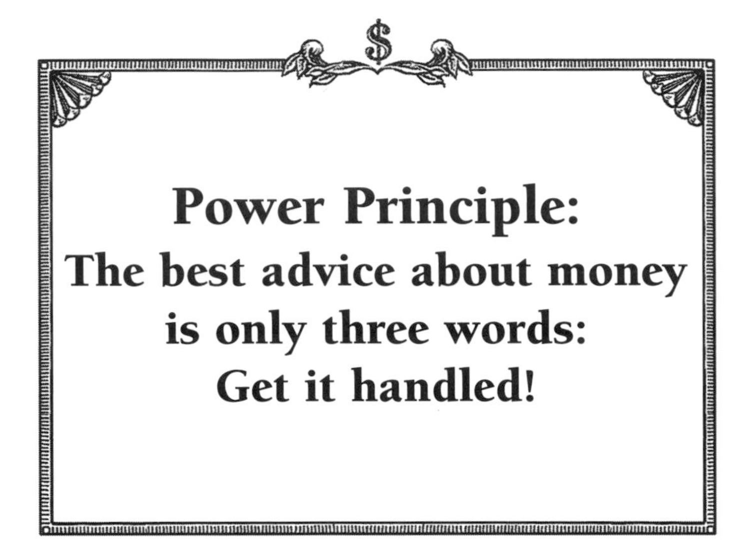

Power Principle:
The best advice about money is only three words: Get it handled!

The fact is, in our society, money is an important TOOL.

Money is like a lubricant — going through life
without it is very, very, rough.

Money doesn't buy happiness, but it can buy FREEDOM: freedom of choice, to be able to do what you enjoy doing and not be forced to do things just because you need "the money."

It's a shame. I have seen far too many good, kind-hearted, talented people, unable to share their unique gifts and talents to the fullest, because they're simply too busy trying to survive. They work long and hard but never get ahead financially. I've said it before and I'll say it again, "If you're going to work hard anyway, you might as well get rich . . . and the quicker the better."

The best advice I ever heard about money was only three words: GET IT HANDLED! And that's what SpeedWealth is all about. It's a proven system that worked for me and can work for you — if you work it. Get the knowledge, master the principles, study the strategies and in just a few years you will never have to worry about money again. You will be free!

It's been an honor to serve you and I hope I can continue to be of support!

For your freedom,

T. Harv Eker

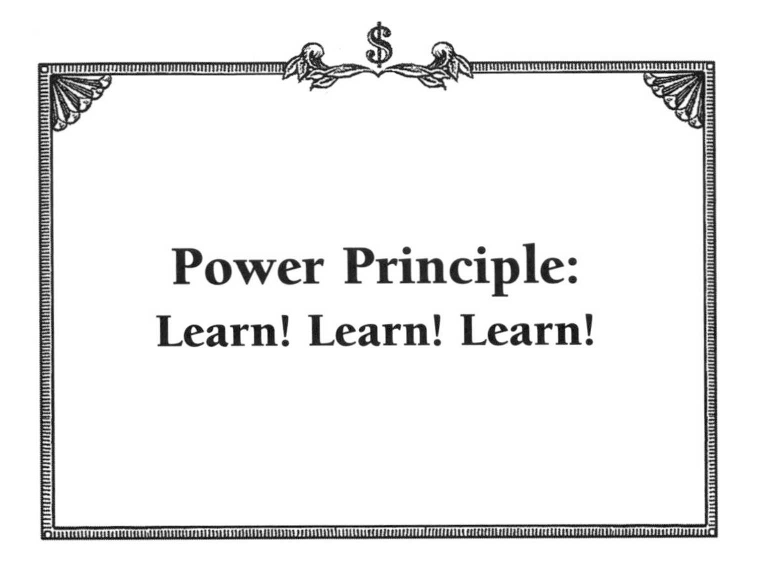

Power Principle:

Learn! Learn! Learn!

A Personal Message From T. Harv Eker

So what do you do now?

Take action! If you're already an "expert" in business and earning at least $250,000 per year, then use this book as a template to enhance the speed of your success. If you're not in this income bracket yet, the best thing you can do is . . .

Learn! Learn! Learn! Remember, success is a learnable skill. If you truly want to succeed you must work on yourself, study business, and become a SpeedWealth master. The wonderful thing about becoming an expert in this game is when you win, you get rich!

Above all, get the knowledge you need, BEFORE you step into the arena. Think about it: if you were going to play Andre Agassi, the great tennis champion, for money, wouldn't you start learning the game and practicing BEFORE you stepped on the court to play him? It amazes me that so many people get into the game of business without acquiring the specific knowledge necessary to win. Then they wonder why they're struggling.

If you're not in your own business yet, this is the time to learn and prepare so when you do "go for it," you'll know what you're doing. If you're already in business and haven't been creating wealth, there's obviously something missing; there's something you don't know. Get the knowledge. Learn the ropes. Apply the SpeedWealth strategies in your business and watch your income skyrocket. That's what I did and it made me a fortune. As you can see, I'm a big believer in education. I love the saying: "If you think education is expensive, try ignorance."

There are three types of education you are going to need if you want to succeed to your fullest potential. One is "general business" knowledge. This would include marketing, negotiations, finance, etc. The next is "business specific" knowledge. This entails learning the "ins and outs" of your particular business. The third and most important is "personal development" knowledge. This allows you to fully utilize the first two types of education. The fact is you can have the greatest "tools" in the world, but if you have a leak in your "toolbox" you're going to have a problem. In short, who are you, how do you think, what are your beliefs, what are your habits, characteristics and traits, how confident are you in yourself? In my experience, all these elements have a dramatic effect on both your success and your happiness. I have a motto that "your income can only grow to the extent that you do." The idea is to grow your "self" and your success will grow naturally and automatically.

To this end, I have created a series of live seminars and tape products designed to help you succeed more quickly, more easily and more happily.

Please see my Peak Potentials Training website for full details at **www.peakpotentials.com**.

Much love,

T. Harv Eker

In the meantime here's a condensed catalog that describes each of our current programs and products:

PEAK POTENTIALS TRAINING

"Inner world principles for real world success"

The Peak Potentials CATALOG

OUR MISSION

To educate and inspire people to live in their higher self, based in courage, purpose and joy versus fear, need and obligation.

PEAK POTENTIALS TRAINING

"Inner world principles for real world success"

"Secrets of the Millionaire Mind *demystifies why some people are destined to be rich while others are destined for a life of struggle. If you want to learn about the root cause of success, read this book."*

- Robert G. Allen, author of *Multiple Streams of Income*

"This is the most powerful, persuasive, and practical book on becoming wealthy you will ever read. It is loaded with ideas, insights, and strategies that will change your thinking and your results forever."

- Brian Tracy, author of *Getting Rich Your Own Way*

Secrets of the Millionaire Mind

"Mastering the Inner Game of Wealth"

#1 NY TIMES BESTSELLER!

Why are some people destined to be rich while others are destined for financial struggle? Find out what makes the difference in this life-changing book.

Secrets of the Millionaire Mind gets to the "root" of financial success! In this groundbreaking book, T. Harv Eker states: "Give me five minutes, and I can predict your financial future for the rest of your life! Even more important, I will show you what you can do to change it almost overnight." Eker does this by identifying your "money and success blueprint." We all have a personal money blueprint, that acts as our financial set point, ingrained in our subconscious minds. It is this blueprint, more than anything, that will determine our financial lives.

You can know everything about marketing, sales, negotiations, stocks, real estate, and the world of finance. If your money blueprint is not set for a high level of success, you will never acquire serious wealth – and if by chance you do, you will most likely lose.

The good news is that now you can actually reset your money blueprint to create natural and automatic success and that's exactly what you will do with the help of this extraordinary book. It's simple. If you think like rich people think and do what rich people do, chances are you'll get rich too!

- **SPECIAL LIMITED TIME BONUS: 2 free tickets to the Millionaire Mind Intensive Seminar (valued at $1295 per person) with each book purchased.**

Get *Secrets of the Millionaire Mind* NOW at your local bookstore or online at www.secretsofthemillionairemind.com

PEAK POTENTIALS TRAINING

"Inner world principles for real world success"

*Contact Peak Potentials for dates, locations and special tuitions. See back page for contact information.

The Millionaire Mind Evening Seminar

"The Secret Psychology of Wealth"

Money miracles can occur when we get out of our own way. The problem is, by ourselves, we can never see what's holding us back from reaching our full potential. Einstein said it best, "You can't solve a problem with the same 'mind' that created it." The information in this course is extremely powerful! If you learn the strategies and use them, your financial life will change forever.

Here's just a portion of what you'll learn:

- The 5 ways rich people think differently than the poor & middle class.
- The hidden cause of almost all financial problems.
- How your childhood conditioning is affecting you financially today.
- Why knowledge and skill do not create wealth.
- How to reset your financial thermostat for 'automatic success'.
- How to create so-called 'luck' and actually attract money.
- How to make your 'mind' work for you instead of against you.

"I am a real estate agent. After the course, in one weekend I closed four deals!" - Debbie Filippelli

"Since the course my income has taken a quantum leap. I have saved more money in the last 10 months than I have in the previous 10 years. Thank you!" - Robert Hall

The Millionaire Mind Intensive 3-Day Workshop

There is a secret psychology to money. Most people don't know about it, that's why most people never become financially successful. We all have a money and success 'blueprint' already ingrained in our subconscious. It comes from past conditioning. The question is what is your blueprint set for – success, mediocrity, failure, struggle, ease, a steady income or the up and down 'yo-yo' effect?

Unfortunately for most people, your current blueprint will stay with you for the rest of your life, unless you identify it and change it. Fortunately, there is a powerful 3-day seminar that will do just that. In it, you will learn how to completely recondition yourself for financial success. For many people, the change will be immediate and permanent.

Here's just a portion of what you'll learn:

- How to win the 'money game' so that you never have to work again.
- The world's easiest, yet most effective money management method.
- The secret to creating multiple streams of passive income.
- The 5 'habits' of truly wealthy people.
- The underlying cause of almost all financial problems.
- How to recondition yourself for automatic and natural success.
- How to master 'money and relationships' (including spouses, business associates and kids).
- How to identify your money personality.
- And much more!

"Your outer world is a reflection of your inner world."

If you're not 100% satisfied with your income, if you're not 100% satisfied with your net worth, if you're stressed out or burnt out, if you're working hard and not getting ahead, if you're not living up to your full potential, then maybe it is time for some new strategies and different ways of thinking. **This program is transformational.** You will not be the same person going out as you were coming in. If you want to blend peace of mind with abundance, join us at the next Millionaire Mind Intensive!

"Since attending your program several months ago, my income has quadrupled. Thanks!" - Sian Lindem

"I'm a waiter and have never earned more than $25,000 a year. three weeks after the workshop I made $14,000 in eight days!"
- Bill Auger

"I had a graphic design business on the verge of closing. Within 60 days of the course, I had so many new clients I had to hire 2 new assistants to help me!" - Kristie Wilson

Enlightened Warrior Training Camp

"How to Access Your True Power and Succeed in Spite of Anything"

For many, life has become more about what they can't do rather than what they can do. The truth, however, is that you are far greater than you 'think' and have truly amazing potential. The key is to tap into your 'higher self' and unleash your full capacity for success and happiness.

This camp is highly experiential. You will not learn 'how to' be an Enlightened Warrior, you will practice 'being' one.

<u>You will discover</u>:

- The secrets to being strong and confident.
- How not to yearn for approval and recognition from others, but to approve of yourself.
- How to respond to circumstances from choice instead of reacting from past conditioning.
- How to live with integrity, so that your word is law.
- How to have the courage to take action in spite of fear, doubt and worry.

The true warrior is "one who conquers oneself".

This course is an inner 'strengthening'. It is an opportunity for you to see yourself in an entirely new light – to meet the absolute best of yourself. The learning is truly transformational and can be applied to all aspects of your everyday life. If you believe there's got to be more to life and are ready to experience an alternative way of living, then commit to your 'self' and do whatever it takes to be there!

Wizard Training Camp

"The Science of Manifesting What You Want"

There is no greater skill than the ability to manifest what you want. This is the magic of the wizard!

The wizard is known as the magician. They are the alchemists, able to turn 'lead into gold.' The unique quality of the wizard is their ability to manifest what they truly want in the real world. There are 7 specific steps to creating anything. At Wizard Training Camp, you will learn and practice this secret science and come away with truly amazing skills that you will use for the rest of your life.

You will learn:

- A highly developed 'reality creation' technology.
- Specific clearing processes to make space for higher wisdom.
- Enlightened principles for creating success without struggle.
- How to tap directly into your intuition.
- How to see through the illusion of the world and come from a higher perspective.

The wizard's way is the way of attraction. The wizard not only succeeds, but does so with elegance and ease.

The Wizard Training is special. If you would like to learn how to manifest exactly what you want in the real world, be there.

Guerrilla Business School

"How to Create Wealth Quickly in any Business you Choose"

This exciting and powerful program is designed to teach you guerrilla business strategies for high-speed success. Whereas most people go into business to make a living, your business will be designed to create wealth and a lifetime of passive income.

Here are just a few of the things you will learn:

- How to generate million-dollar ideas every 60 seconds!
- How to make or save a fortune using guerrilla negotiation tactics.
- How to raise $10,000 to 1/2 a million dollars without asking anyone to finance anything.
- How to start any business or division with little or no money down.
- Become a marketing genius in 6 hours flat.
- How to get the best people working for you for half of what they would normally charge and be thrilled about it.
- Win-win sales strategies that work in the real world.
- How to set up your business for massive passive income or sell it for millions if you choose to.
- And much more!

All taught using high-impact processes, games, experiential exercises, case studies, hot seats, and makeovers. This program will be taught by T. Harv Eker and several other millionaire business owners.

Using what you learn at Guerrilla Business School, you will quit wasting time with strategies that produce little or mediocre results and begin creating wealth in any business you choose for the rest of your life.

I have a double major in International Business and Marketing from the second-ranked business school in the world, plus over 10 years of real-world business experience – this course completely blew it out of the water. I currently make over $1 million per year and now plan on making over $100 million over the next 2-3 years.

- Rick Grunden

Amazing! This course brings the masters together and illustrates, hands-on, how to implement successful techniques into the market place. It's worth ten times the value.

- Jason Labrecque

Life Directions Intensive

"Discover Your Personal Mission and Create a Successful Vision"

"The #1 reason most people don't get what they want is... they don't know what they want." **- T. Harv Eker**

Do you ever feel that you could do anything - if you just knew what it was? Nothing is worse than not having a clear direction. Without a clear direction, you are either paralyzed or busy running around in circles.

Each of us is unique and different. Each of us has something special to offer the world. Each of us has our own natural gifts and talents. To truly be happy, we must use our gifts to add value to the lives of others. However, it is also important to be financially successful. To be happy, you need money and meaning.

The objective of Life Directions is to help you create a vehicle that expresses who you are and why you are here in a way that is successful in the real world.

The course includes:

- Discovering your own life purpose and your personal life mission.
- How to absolutely know your true passion.
- How a mid-life 'crisis' is really a mid-life 'calling'.
- How to make decisions that align your head and your heart.
- How to make choices based in joy and purpose versus fear and obligation.

- How to find a business or career that expresses your gifts and allows you to create wealth.
- A step-by-step blueprint for making your vision a reality.

By the end of this program, you will re-ignite your passion for living. You will know your true purpose and mission in life. You will find a business or career vehicle that expresses your special gifts. You will know exactly how to make this vehicle financially successful. You will have an immediate and long-term action plan. You will own the skill to fine-tune, revise or even change your life direction anytime you desire, for the rest of your life!

Einstein said it best, ***"A life without cause is a life without effect."*** If you are sick and tired of 'searching' and want to start 'finding,' this course will change your life!

"Train The Trainer" Certification

"How to Earn $20,000 a Weekend Teaching What You Love!"

Being a trainer can be one of the most exciting and fulfilling professions on the planet, but if you're missing some critical knowledge and skills, it can be a major struggle. Most people in the training and speaking arena are poor presenters and don't make any money! The secret to success in this business is to learn from the masters – people who speak to groups of hundreds or thousands at a time and consistently earn massive amounts of money.

The only problem is that most trainers in this category would never reveal their innermost secrets to success and the psychology behind every move they make. T. Harv Eker and his master team of facilitators, will. You will learn and experience everything you need to know about becoming a truly amazing presenter. You will come away knowing exactly how to earn a fortune teaching what you love.

The Train The Trainer Certification program will increase your confidence in this arena by a thousand-fold. You'll be shockingly surprised at what you can do once you've been properly educated in the intricacies of this field.

Here is just a portion of what you will learn:

- How to earn up to $20,000 a weekend or more!
- Designing a powerful program from A-Z.
- How to control the energy in the room.
- A proven blueprint to market your seminars and yourself as a speaker/trainer.

- How to use 'Accelerated Learning' techniques so your participants learn faster and remember more.
- A step-by-step process for getting started and earning money immediately.

This program can and will change your life – both from a perspective of personal and professional development and also from a financial point of view.

"It's always been my intention to 'teach teachers' who will go out and make a real difference in this world." **- T. Harv Eker**

Wealth & Wisdom

"World-Class Experts Reveal How to Create More Money, Love, and Happiness in Your Life!"

Learning is critical to success but 'who' you learn from makes all the difference in the world! At Wealth & Wisdom, several of the top authors and trainers in North America will come together to teach you the skills of business, money, relationships and happiness at one of the most incredible business and personal development events ever held in North America. Guest trainers have included Dr. Wayne Dyer, Richard Carlson, Robert G. Allen, Cheri Huber, Jack Canfield, Jay Abraham and John Kehoe.

Each training session will be a complete workshop where you will learn specific skills you can benefit from immediately and use for the rest of your life.

The Wealth & Wisdom conference is not to be missed.

The SuccessTracs Coaching Program

"Double Your Income, Double Your Time Off and Double Your Speed to Financial Freedom!"

There are only 2 elements to success, 'knowing what to do' and 'doing what you know.' The SuccessTracs Coaching Program ensures that you will do both. SuccessTracs is an on-going learning and coaching process that will gently 'force' you to succeed. We use live seminars, teleconferences, audio tapes, and tracking systems to help you clarify and achieve your objectives in every area of your life.

The object of the program is for you to at least double your income, double your time off, and double your speed to financial freedom! In this program you will learn and master the critical elements of business, financial, and personal success. You will also enjoy structured networking with positive, like-minded people.

The SuccessTracs Program features a revolutionary 'time system' whereby you will become more effective with your time and learn to 'work smarter, not harder.' You will dramatically increase your productivity, organization, and free time.

Our SuccessTracs members are achieving phenomenal results in their businesses, their finances, and their level of happiness.

If your results are not matching your potential, join the SuccessTracs program today.

"If you could do it on your own, chances are you would have already done it." **- T. Harv Eker**

PEAK POTENTIALS TRAINING

"Inner world principles for real world success"

Visit our WEBSITE for details and special pricing on the following products at **www.peakpotentials.com**

SpeedWealth™

"How To Make A Million In Your Own Business In 3 Years Or Less"

Best-selling Book

SpeedWealth™ Seminar

CD's. Recorded Live!

SpeedWealth™ for Network Marketers

CD's. Recorded Live!

The SpeedWealth Masters Camp

"13 Masters Teach You a Step-By-Step System for Becoming a Millionaire in 3 Years or Less"

CD's. Recorded Live!

The Millionaire Mind Evening

An Introduction to the Principles of the "Millionaire Mind"

CD's or Video. Recorded Live!

The Millionaire Mind Intensive

"The Secret Psychology of Wealth"

CD's. Recorded Live!

Enlightened Wealth Training

"Mastering Money, Business and Happiness"

CD's. Recorded Live!

Wealth & Wisdom Series

World Class Experts Reveal . . .
"How to Create More Money, Love, and Happiness in Your Life"

CD's. Recorded Live!

Millionaire School Series

Financial experts reveal the inside edge to wealth and investment strategies.

CD's. Recorded Live!

The MasterMind Tape Series

"Secrets of Success" from North America's top authors and trainers.

CD's. Recorded Live!

Peak Potentials' Clothing

ON SALE NOW!

Visit...

www.peakpotentials.com

PEAK POTENTIALS TRAINING

"Inner world principles for real world success"

Now you can have T. Harv Eker give an exciting presentation to your group. Eker has been called, "one of the freshest, most dynamic speakers in North America." He blends wit with wisdom, playfulness with power and "street-smarts" with heart. Eker ignites audiences with his passion and his enthusiasm is contagious, yet the comment most often expressed about him is that he is "real." T. Harv Eker serves up a rare combination of immediately useable information with long-lasting inspiration! Topic lengths range from 1 hour to 2 days, depending on your objectives.

TOPICS INCLUDE:

- **SpeedWealth™** "How To Make A Million In Your Own Business In 3 Years or Less!"
- **SpeedWealth™** for Network Marketers "How To Make A Million In Your Network Marketing Business In 3 Years or Less!"
- **The Millionaire Mind™** "The Secret Psychology of Wealth"
- **Breakthrough to Power** "How to Master Your Mind for Success" (Including the amazing "arrow-break" demonstration)
- **Becoming the Ultimate Success Warrior** "How To Succeed In Spite of Anything"
- **Enlightened Business** "Using the 7 Traits of Your 'Higher Self' at Work"
- **The Science of Manifestation** "How to Create What You Want"
- **Success Without Stress** "How to Stay Centered, Calm and Peaceful Regardless of Any Circumstance"
- **Secrets of the Millionaire Mind™** "Mastering the Inner Game of Wealth"

To order or for further details...

call: **(604) 983-3344**

fax: **(604) 983-3564**

email:

programs@peakpotentials.com

or visit our website at:

www.peakpotentials.com

Peak Potentials Training
1651 Welch Street
North Vancouver, BC V7P 3G9
Canada

Phone: (604) 983-3344
Fax: (604) 983-3564

Email: programs@peakpotentials.com
Website: www.peakpotentials.com